ÉCRINS NATIONAL PARK

ABOUT THE AUTHOR

KEV REYNOLDS, author of this guide, is a freelance writer, photojournalist and lecturer whose first title for Cicerone Press (*Walks and Climbs in the Pyrenees*) appeared in 1978 and is still in print. He has published many books on the Alps, a series of trekkers' guides to the Nepal Himalaya and, nearer to home, several books on walking in Southern England. A member of the Alpine Club, Austrian Alpine Club and Outdoor Writers' Guild, his enthusiasm for mountains in particular, and the countryside in general, remains undiminished after 40 years of activity. Living among what he calls the 'Kentish Alps', he regularly travels around Britain to share that enthusiasm through his lectures.

Cicerone guidebooks by Kev Reynolds

Walking in the Alps
100 Hut Walks in the Alps
Tour of the Vanoise
Chamonix to Zermatt, Walkers' Haute Route
Alpine Pass Route
The Valais
The Bernese Alps
Ticino – Switzerland
Walks in the Engadine – Switzerland
Central Switzerland
The Jura (with R.B. Evans)
Walks & Climbs in the Pyrenees
Everest – a Trekker's Guide

Annapurna – a Trekker's Guide
Langtang & Helambu – a Trekker's Guide
Kangchenjunga – a Trekker's Guide
Manaslu – a Trekker's Guide
Walking in Kent Vols I & II
Walking in Sussex
The South Downs Way & North Downs Way
The Wealdway & The Vanguard Way
The Cotswold Way

ÉCRINS NATIONAL PARK

(FRENCH ALPS)

A Walking Guide

by

Kev Reynolds

CICERONE PRESS
MILNTHORPE CUMBRIA
www.cicerone.co.uk

ISBN 1 85284 322 5
A catalogue record for this book is available from the British Library

DEDICATION

For my wife, with love, and to mark some great days we've
shared in the Alps.

ACKNOWLEDGEMENTS

Thanks are due once more to my publishers at Cicerone Press for
adding this title to their growing list of guidebooks to the Alps, and
for providing me with another excuse to spend weeks of activity
among these spectacular mountains. John Brailsford, mountain
guide and author of the Alpine Club climber's guide to the Écrins
Massif, initially drew my attention to the splendours of the region,
which a solo backpacking journey round the Tour of the Oisans
subsequently verified. My wife accompanied me during the first
research trip for this book, and my old climbing and trekking partner
Alan Payne shared some of the routes during the second. Thanks to
both for adding significantly to my daily enjoyment of the hills. I am
grateful also to Marie-Claude Turc of La Cordée in St-Christophe for
hospitality and advice, and to the many hut wardens and tourist
office staff who gave useful suggestions. All helped to make research
for this book a constant delight.

Kev Reynolds

Advice to Readers

Readers are advised that while every effort is taken by
the author to ensure the accuracy of this guidebook,
changes can occur which may affect the contents. It is
advisable to check locally on transport, accommodation,
shops, etc, but even rights of way can be altered.

The publisher would welcome notes of any such
changes.

CONTENTS

VALLÉE DU VÉNÉON

ÉCRINS NATIONAL PARK

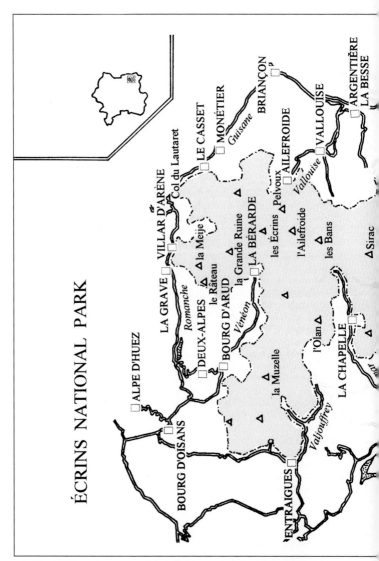

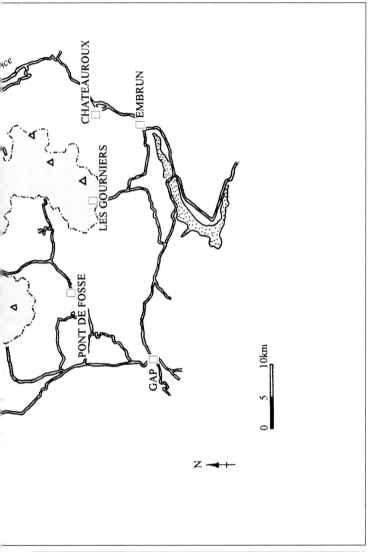

CHATEAUROUX

EMBRUN

LES GOURNIERS

PONT DE FOSSE

GAP

N

0   5   10km

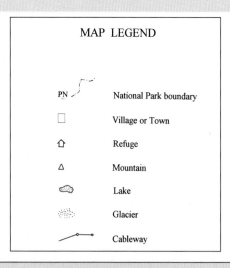

MAP LEGEND

PN	National Park boundary
☐	Village or Town
⇧	Refuge
△	Mountain
◯	Lake
⋯	Glacier
⟋—◦—•	Cableway

International Distress Signal
(Only to be used in an emergency)

Six blasts on a whistle (and flashes with a torch after dark) spaced
evenly for one minute, followed by a minute's pause.
Repeat until an answer is received. The response is three signals
per minute followed by a minute's pause.

The following signals are used to communicate with a helicopter:

Help needed:
raise both arms
above head to
form a 'V'

Help not required:
raise one arm above
head, extend other
arm downward

In an emergency the mountain rescue (*secours en montagne*)
can be called on 04 92 22 22 22
Note: mountain rescues must be paid for – be insured

INTRODUCTION

Variously known as the Écrins, Oisans, Haut Dauphiné or Massif du Pelvoux, the area covered by this guidebook is arguably one of the most visually spectacular in all the Alps. Hung about with glaciers, more than 100 peaks rise to well over 3000m (the Barre des Écrins, which gives its name to the area, is 4102m), while in several valleys rock walls soar to jagged summits too steep to contain either permanent snow or ice. Not surprisingly, for well over 100 years the Massif des Écrins has attracted climbers at the top end of the sport with its wealth of routes – both rock, and snow and ice – of the highest standard.

But as that great Alpine connoisseur R.L.G. Irving once noted: 'The Dauphiné Alps have things to offer besides glacier and precipice. Some of the pastures that surround the central chaos of high peaks have long been celebrated for their flowers, especially those behind La Grave and around the Col du Lautaret.'

He should also have mentioned the walks, for despite the severity of the mountains and the depths of the valleys, there are hundreds of kilometres of well-marked trails that lead to open plateaux sprinkled with tarns, or to valley basins caught in rocky horseshoes of impressive grandeur, to mountain huts or waterfalls or walkers' passes linking valley systems, Alp hamlets, villages and Irving's pastures celebrated for their flowers. No one who enjoys wild mountain scenery, and has the energy and inclination to explore on foot, could possibly grow tired of the Écrins, and this guidebook is a celebration of the savage beauty revealed by way of its footpaths.

THE VALLEYS OF THE ÉCRINS

Located southeast of Grenoble and unequally split between the *départements* of Isère and Hautes-Alpes, the Parc National des Écrins is the largest in France, covering an area of 92,000 hectares (227,332 acres), with a peripheral zone nearly twice that size. This is

AREAS COVERED

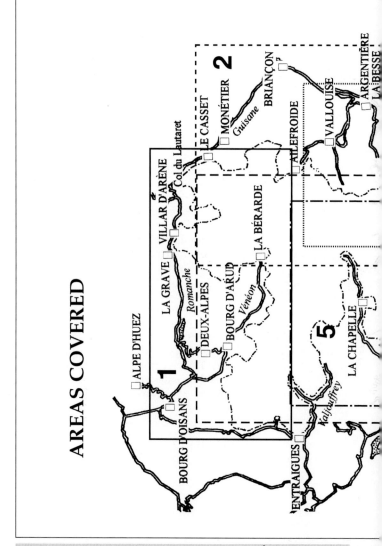

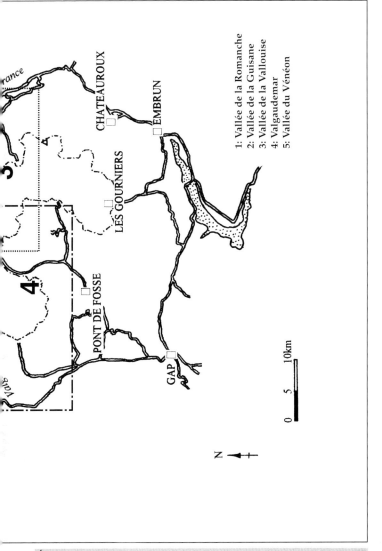

1: Vallée de la Romanche
2: Vallée de la Guisane
3: Vallée de la Vallouise
4: Valgaudemar
5: Vallée du Vénéon

mountain country par excellence, with the highest peaks forming a block at the very heart of the range, and a diverse assortment of valleys surrounding or spreading from it. Beginning in the north, and travelling clockwise around the national park, the most important of these valleys are as follows.

Vallée de la Romanche

One of the region's main access routes between Grenoble and Briançon via Col du Lautaret journeys through the Vallée de la Romanche along the Park's northern rim. At its western end Bourg d'Oisans makes a good base, for it's conveniently situated close to a junction of valleys (the Vénéon lies to the southeast) and has good public transport connections. However, the best walking opportunities lie further east, in the vicinity of La Grave and Villar d'Arène at the foot of the Lautaret road, with the Meije bursting out of the valley to the south and an impressive group of high mountains clustered nearby. Trails lead among and below these peaks, visiting remote huts and wild inner glens inhabited by marmot and chamois. The more gentle country north of the Romanche, whilst lying outside the national park, also has countless walking routes, with glorious views to the big mountains on the far side of the valley. The multi-day Tour of the Oisans, which follows GR54 on a circuit of the northern and central Écrins, begins and ends in Bourg d'Oisans, travels along that northern hillside and comes down to La Grave before heading southeast across Col d'Arsine to gain Le Casset in the Vallée de la Guisane.

Vallée de la Guisane

Descending from Col du Lautaret to Briançon (claimed to be Europe's highest town), the Guisane skirts the northeastern edge of the national park and gives only a few distant hints of its glacial heartland. The upper part of the valley is bounded by some rugged rock scenery, the middle section is more broad and open, while in the lower third the resort of Serre Chevalier (which encompasses several small resorts) is the largest winter sports complex in the Southern Alps. Created in 1941 it is now equipped with something like 70 lifts which edge close to the Park's eastern border, but these lifts are happily restricted from straying over it. In summer, when

La Grave is visited along a number of routes in the Vallée de la Romanche

there is no skiable snow, the Serre-Chevalier *téléphérique*, which rises to 2491m, can be used to gain access to a series of high trails that follow ridge crests or descend into neighbouring valleys. Downstream from the Serre Chevalier resort Briançon, on the other hand, is an historic attraction situated at a confluence of rivers in the valley of the Durance. This valley flows south and remains some distance east of the Parc National des Écrins. But at the village of Argentière-la-Bessée a road breaks away northwest along the Vallée de la Vallouise leading to the rugged heart of the region.

Vallée de la Vallouise

There are two main centres here: the little market town of Vallouise, and Ailefroide, which is one of the two major climbing centres of the Écrins region (the other being La Bérarde). Though both lie at a junction of valleys, Vallouise is open and sunny, while Ailefroide is confined between huge rock walls, and with forest crowding its outskirts. At the head of the Vallée de la Vallouise there's a broad open plain known as the Pré de Madame Carle. The rubble-strewn Glacier Noir drains down towards it from the west, but above big glacial slabs in the north the tumbling Glacier Blanc gleams in the sunlight. Both entice with prospects of scenically-exciting walks among the highest of the high peaks. Despite Ailefroide's reputation as a major climbing centre, it also makes a near-perfect base for a walking holiday, and this guidebook gives a number of first-rate outings from it. As for Vallouise, this has the tributary valley of the Onde stretching off to the west which offers good walking too, as well as footpaths in the main valley and in that of Chambran to the north.

Valgaudemar

On the western side of the Parc National two main valleys cut into the range with access from the N85 Grenoble–Gap road. The south-ernmost of these is the Valgaudemar. La Chapelle-en-Valgaudemar is the modest base here, located just 9km from the roadhead. The huge rock peak of L'Olan rises north of the village, and there's a narrow glen cutting back to the south. At the head of the valley a mountain cirque provides plenty of scope for walks to huts, tarns and viewpoints, and accommodation is supplied in this upper valley by the streamside Refuge du Clot, as well as the large Chalet-Hôtel du Gioberney at the roadhead.

Valjouffrey

This northernmost valley on the western side of the Écrins park is watered by the Bonne river which drains west of L'Olan. Road access is from La Mure on N85, with a modest amount of accom-modation to be had at Valbonnais in the lower valley, at Entraigues at the confluence of the Malsanne and Bonne, and, for the trekker tackling the Tour of the Oisans, at Le Désert. Upstream beyond Le Désert the valley has been carved and shaped by a long-departed glacier; waterfalls spray down the steep walls, and nestling at the foot of L'Olan is the Fond-Turbat refuge. Below Le Désert at La Chapelle-en-Valjoufrey, the tributary glen of Valsenestre carves northeastward through the Gorges de Béranger, with a minor road ending at Valsenestre hamlet – another staging post on the Tour of the Oisans. Then, at Entraigues in the mouth of the Malsanne valley, the D526 offers a rather tortuous cross-country road route to Bourg d'Oisans via Col d'Ornon.

Vallée du Vénéon

The final entry in our summary of valleys is the Vénéon, which rises in the glacial heartland of the massif and flows roughly northwest out to the Romanche a short distance upstream of Bourg d'Oisans. The Vénéon is a gem of a valley fed by a number of attractive tributary glens, all of which are well worth exploring on foot. An infrequent daily bus service runs from Bourg to La Bérarde, the final village situated at the roadhead where the upper Vénéon is joined by the Etançons torrent – the latter draining glaciers on the south side of La Meije. Within the valley there are several small centres, but no real resorts. Naming from west to east these are: Venosc, Bourg d'Arud, St-Christophe-en-Oisans and La Bérarde, the 'Chamonix' (in terms of mountaineering appeal) of the Écrins.

THE PARC NATIONAL DES ÉCRINS

In 1913 a protected zone was centred on La Bérarde, but it took another 60 years before the Parc National des Écrins came fully into being as the fifth, but largest, such national park in France. Vauban had once described the region as having 'mountains reaching for the sky, and valleys sinking to incredible depths'. And it is just such a landscape that is characteristic of the Park.

In the north and west the mountains consist of crystalline and metamorphic rocks (granite and gneiss), while sedimentary rocks (limestone, schist and clay) dominate in the south and east. There's a surprisingly large number of glaciers amounting to some 17,000 hectares, for the Dauphiné Alps is the southernmost region of the Alpine chain to retain ice-sheets of any size, and it is largely due to the powerful rivers and waterfalls flowing from them that such deep valleys and gorges have been cut.

The extraordinary difference in elevation between valley bed and mountain summit, ranging from 800m to 4000m, coupled with oceanic influences in the north and west, and Mediterranean influences in the south, are responsible for the wonderfully rich and diverse flora of the Écrins. Some 1800 species have been identified within the Park (that's half of all French flora); 800 of these are protected, while around 40 are considered either rare or endangered, and 35 are endemic to the area.

As for wildlife, the Park lists 64 species of mammal, including typical Alpine favourites such as ibex, chamois and marmot. The ibex was reintroduced to the Écrins as recently as 1990–1995, but the chamois is well-established and the population now numbers around 12,000. There are 210 species of nesting birds and the largest concentration of Golden Eagles in France, while the Bearded Vulture is a regular visitor.

In keeping with its status as an area of conservation and environmental protection, the national park has a list of regulations which the visitor should observe. These are summarised below:

- Dogs are not allowed, even on a lead. Respect wildlife and livestock.
- Do not pick or take samples of plants, rocks and fossils, or animals.
- Firearms are banned, and all wildlife within the national park is protected.
- Leave no litter. Keep the countryside clean.
- Do not light fires.
- Avoid making unnecessary noise.
- Off-site camping is restricted to an overnight pitch between 7pm and 9am, at least one hour's walk from a road or the Park boundary.
- Motor vehicles and bicycles are only allowed on authorized roads.

GETTING THERE

Assuming one approaches from the north and west, Grenoble is the key to entry to the whole region no matter what the method of travel.

By Air

Daily scheduled flights operate from Paris to Grenoble-Saint-Geoirs and Lyon-Satolas. Fly-drive arrangements are available via airlines and tour operators, but note that the minimum age for hiring a car in France varies from 21 to 25 years, depending on the hire company. Some companies levy a surcharge on drivers below 25 years of age.

By Train

For anyone travelling direct from the UK the train is a convenient option. Eurostar takes three hours for the journey from London Waterloo to Paris (Gare du Nord) via the Channel Tunnel, and the high-speed (300 km/h) TGV service connects Paris (Gare de Lyon) with Grenoble in 2hrs 55mins. There are also main-line services from Paris to Briançon. A range of special reduced-rate tickets and rail passes are available. Enquiries to the Rail Europe Travel Centre, 179 Piccadilly, London W1V 0BA (☎ 0990 203 7000; calls are charged at the national rate). In France reservations and information can be obtained from Grenoble (☎ 08 36 35 35 35).

By Coach

Regular coach services operated by Eurolines take about 16 hours for the journey from London (Victoria Coach Station) to Grenoble. This is the cheapest method of scheduled public transport between the UK and the Alps. Contact your local National Express agent for information and bookings, or visit Eurolines office at 52 Grosvenor Gardens, London SW1W 0AW (☎ 08705 143219   Website: www.eurolines.co.uk).

Local Bus Information

Local buses operate out of Grenoble (the Gare routière is adjacent to the mainline railway station) with the following destinations: Gap, La Mure, Bourg d'Oisans, Briançon, etc. Connecting VFD buses for several other destinations such as La Bérarde, Alpe d'Huez, etc, have Bourg d'Oisans as their terminus.

Grenoble–Bourg d'Oisans: VFD Gare routière de Bourg d'Oisans (☎ 04 76 80 00 90)
Grenoble–Briançon/Grenoble-Gap: VFD Gare routière de Grenoble (☎ 04 76 87 90 31)
Grenoble–Gap/Gap–Briançon: Société des Cars Alpes Littoral (SCAL), 1 cours Ladoucette, 05000 GAP (☎ 04 92 51 06 05)

By Car

The journey from the Channel ports to Grenoble is straightforward by autoroute via Paris, but note that these are toll roads and are therefore reasonably expensive to use. The road distance from

Calais to Grenoble is about 830km. In France the minimum driving age is 18. Nationals of European Union countries need a valid driving licence, while those from non-EU countries require an international driving licence. The vehicle's log book should be carried, and insurance cover is compulsory. Front-seat passengers must wear seat-belts, and children below the age of ten are restricted to the back seat.

ACCOMMODATION

A variety of accommodation is on offer throughout the region, from campsites to all but the most elegant of hotels. Outline details are given within the main body of this guide, but for specific information you are advised to contact the local tourist offices who can usually supply printed lists of hotels, *gîtes* and campsites, and provide an idea of prices. (Details of tourist offices are given at the start of each valley section.)

Official Campsites
Campsites of varying sizes are located in most of the main valleys – but not in all of them. Every one used personally during research had good, clean and efficient facilities. However, as with other forms of accommodation, beware that they can be very busy during the main summer holiday period, which in France begins on 14 July and continues until late August.

Gîtes d'étape
Gîtes may be described as privately-owned youth hostels predominantly used by walkers. Although some have small bedrooms, most sleeping accommodation is in dormitories (take your own sheet sleeping bag). Bathrooms have showers, and there's a communal kitchen where guests prepare their own meals, but a number of *gîte* owners serve evening meals and breakfasts to supplement their income. There are more than 60 *gîtes d'étape* in the Écrins region.

Mountain Huts (Refuges)
Throughout the Écrins, mountain huts are often completely full during the French summer holiday period, and it is essential to

phone ahead if you plan to use one for overnight lodging. There are many such huts within the national park, and a number of routes in this guide lead to them, for almost every one has been built in an idyllic location. Sleeping arrangements are invariably in dormitories with large communal bunks with up to 30 places. There is no segregation of the sexes, and washroom facilities are usually quite basic and often without hot water. The *gardien* (where one is in residence) will normally provide cooked meals and sell bottled drinks, coffee and tea. Snacks and drinks are usually on sale during the day for passing walkers. Details of individual huts within the region covered by this guide are given in the appropriate sections.

Hotels

In the region covered by this guide, hotels are mostly small and modestly priced with a limited number of rooms. Although there are no major resorts, a number of unpretentious villages boast a one- or two-star hotel offering accommodation with a distinctly rural mountain atmosphere.

WEATHER

As with all Alpine areas, weather conditions here are changeable and walkers should be prepared for all contingencies. So far as walking is concerned, summer is limited to the period July to mid-September, but while daytime temperatures can be very pleasant during settled conditions, perhaps ranging from 25°C to 28°C, it is possible to encounter heavy rain and even snowfall in midsummer. Even in high summer nights can be cool. Thunderstorms can occur during unsettled periods, and these can be sudden and violent. September is often marked by more settled weather than July or August, but with lower temperatures.

Average daytime temperatures (in °C) for the Dauphiné Alps are as follows:

Jan	Feb	Mar	Apr	May	Jun	Jul	Aug	Sept	Oct	Nov	Dec
3.1	3.7	7.9	13.8	15.7	22.4	26.8	25.7	22.7	15.9	10.7	6.3

Always check the weather forecast (*metéo*) before setting out on a walk that will take you high in the mountains. The local tourist office or Bureau des Guides usually display a printed forecast covering a two- or three-day period. Alternatively, telephone 08 36 68 02 38.

Remember that what is a gentle breeze in the valley may be a piercing wind just 300m up the hillside, and as you gain height so the weather intensifies. Should a passing cloud hide the sun, the temperature can drop alarmingly. As a general guide, the temperature drops about 6°C for every 1000m of ascent.

Violent gusts of wind often indicate that a thunder storm is imminent. Lightning can be deadly and in the mountains the electrical atmosphere preceding a strike sometimes sounds like a swarm of bees. If there's any possibility of a storm, avoid ridges, metallic fixtures and prominent features that stand above open ground. Do not shelter beneath overhanging rocks or trees, and should you be caught in high open country discard metal objects (trekking pole or ice axe), and squat or curl up on your rucksack keeping hands and bare parts of your body away from the rock surface.

NOTES FOR WALKERS

Walks described in this guide have been chosen with a particular hut, lake, pass or viewpoint being the goal, while the principal objective of each outing is to enjoy a day's (or half-day's) exercise among some of the finest mountain scenery in France. But to gain the most from such a holiday one needs to be in reasonably good physical condition, so do try to get fit before travelling to the Alps. Then you will not be daunted by a steep and seemingly endless uphill trail, and the first day of the holiday can be as enjoyable as the last.

Avoid being over-ambitious for the first few days, especially if you've never walked in the Alps before. It's better to increase height gain and distance steadily as you grow accustomed to the scale of these mountains – which initially may seem quite daunting. A range of walks has been chosen, so there should be something for everyone. They fall into three categories, graded 1–3, with the highest grade denoting the more challenging routes. However, this grading system is purely subjective, and newcomers to the Alps

Villar d'Arène: a base for walking in the Vallée de la Romanche

(particularly at the start of a holiday) might consider a Grade 2 outing serious enough. There are moderate walks (Grade 1) that would appeal to all active members of a family, but the majority of routes described are graded 2 or 3, largely resulting from the severity of the landscape.

Within the Parc National des Écrins most paths are well maintained and waymarking adequate to good, but some of the more adventurous routes cross terrain where trails are non-existent beyond a vague line of cairns. In such places it is essential to remain alert and observant in order to avoid becoming lost – especially in poor visibility. If in doubt about the onward route, return to the last point where you were certain of your whereabouts and try again. If you consult the map frequently during the walk you should be able to keep abreast of your position and anticipate junctions before reaching them.

• Check the weather forecast before setting out (see above). Be aware that all Alpine areas are subject to rapidly-changing conditions, and throughout the day watch for tell-tale signs and be prepared with appropriate clothing.

- When starting out on a full-day's walk carry food (including emergency rations such as chocolate or dried fruit) and at least one litre of liquid per person to avoid dehydration.

- Leave details of your planned route and expected time of return with a responsible person, or (if you have your own transport) leave a note with such details visible in your car.

- Be vigilant when crossing wet rocks, scree, snow patches and mountain streams. If you come to a section of path safeguarded by fixed ropes or chains, check that they have not worked loose before relying on them.

- Do not stray onto glaciers unless you have experience, companions and the necessary equipment to deal with crevasse rescue. Keep away from icefalls and hanging glaciers.

- Avoid dislodging stones onto others who might be below you.

- Never be reluctant to turn back in face of deteriorating weather or if the route becomes hazardous. In the event of your being unable to reach the place where you're expected, try to send a message.

- Carry map and compass with you – and know how to use them.

- Always carry some first aid equipment, as well as a whistle and torch for use in emergencies. The emergency telephone number for mountain rescue (*secours en montagne*) is: 04 92 22 22 22. Try not to use it!

- Make a note of the International Distress Signal, which is six blasts on a whistle (and flashes with a torch after dark) followed by a minute's silence. Then repeat until an answer is received. The reply is three signals followed by a minute's pause.

- Be insured against accidents (rescue and subsequent medical treatment), for although mountain rescue here is highly efficient, it can be very expensive for the casualty. (See Appendix C for addresses of specialist mountain insurance companies.)

- And finally, please help to keep the mountains and their valleys litter-free. Carry a spare plastic bag in your rucksack for any leftover cans, bottles and food wrappers, and dispose of them properly in your valley base.

SUGGESTED EQUIPMENT LIST

Experienced hill walkers will no doubt have their own preferences, but for newcomers to the Alps the following list is offered as a guide. Some items will clearly not be needed if you only envisage tackling low valley walks.

Clothing:
- Walking boots – must be comfortable, well fitting, with ankle support and plenty of grip in the soles
- Trainers or similar for wear in huts, hotels and villages
- Wind- and water-proof jacket and overtrousers
- Umbrella
- Woollen hat and sunhat
- Gloves
- Fleece or woollen sweater
- Shirts – 2 or 3 for a fortnight's holiday
- Warm long trousers, slacks or breeches – not jeans which are very cold when wet
- Shorts (optional)
- Long woollen socks
- Underwear

Miscellaneous:
- Rucksack – with waterproof liner and/or cover
- Sheet sleeping bag (if you plan to stay in huts)
- Bivvy bag – in case of emergencies
- Trekking pole(s) – very useful on steep descents, scree, snow, stream crossings, etc
- Headtorch plus spare batteries and bulbs
- Water bottle (minimum 1 litre)
- Sunglasses, suncream/sunblock and lip salve
- First aid kit
- Map and compass
- Whistle
- Watch
- Guidebook

- Penknife
- Camera and films
- Binoculars
- Altimeter

RECOMMENDED MAPS

All the walks included in this guide may be followed using just one map: Didier Richard sheet number 6, published under the heading *Écrins Haut-Dauphiné* at a scale of 1:50,000 (1cm = 500m or roughly 1¼" = 1mile). This may be obtained from major map stockists in the UK (addresses given in Appendix C), and is available in most valley centres within the Écrins region.

Didier Richard maps are based on the official IGN survey (Institut Géographique National – equivalent to the Ordnance Survey in the UK), with the addition of major walking routes highlighted in blue, and mountain huts and *gîtes d'étape* made prominent with a red outline and red lettering. The cartography is very good, and the amount of detail shown is perfectly adequate for the walker's needs. Altitudes and distances quoted in this guidebook are generally based on this particular sheet (1996 edition), although where the map is at variance with either mountaineering convention (in respect of the height of some summits) or the altitude of certain huts, I have made a judgement based on either conventional prejudice or the reading on my own altimeter during research.

For walkers who prefer the greater detail shown on 1:25,000 scale maps (1cm = 250m or roughly 2½" = 1 mile), the IGN publishes no less than six sheets to cover the same area. Headed TOP 25, these are: 3535 OT *Névache*; 3536 OT *Briançon*; 3435 ET *Valloire*; 3436 ET *Meije-Pelvoux*; 3335 ET *Le Bourg d'Oisans-L'Alpe d'Huez*; and 3336 ET *Les 2 Alpes*.

Note: IGN TOP 25 maps are being allocated a UTM-WGS 84 grid to enable the position given by a GPS receiver to be easily localised on the map.

USING THE GUIDE

The layout of this guide follows a clockwise circuit round the Parc National des Écrins from valley to valley. Each major valley system is treated within one section (or chapter) in which a number of walks of various grades are described. All the walks are listed in the index at the end of the book. As mentioned above, the grading system ranges from 1 to 3, with the lowest number referring to the easiest and/or shortest walks, Grade 2 for moderate and medium length outings, and Grade 3 given for the longer and more demanding routes. However, this simplistic system will inevitably have variations and (no doubt) a few anomalies which may be disputed by users of this book, but they are offered in good faith and as a rough guide only.

Distances are quoted throughout in kilometres and metres, as are heights. (Metric conversions are given in Appendix D.) As mentioned above, these details are mostly taken from the map, but in attempting to measure the actual distance of each walk it was necessary to make the nearest estimation I could – with countless zigzags on many routes, it's impossible to be precise.

The time given for each route refers only to **actual walking time** and makes no allowances for rest stops or interruptions for photography – such stops can add considerably to the overall period of activity, so bear this in mind when planning your day. Times are, of course, approximations only, and each walker will have his own pace which may or may not agree with that quoted. By comparing your times with those given here, you should soon have a reasonable idea of how much we differ and compensate accordingly.

A number of the day routes described follow individual stages of the long distance GR54 (Tour of the Ossians). See Appendix A for more information on the GR54 in relation to the routes in this book.

GENERAL INFORMATION

Currency and Exchange

At the time of writing the franc is the national currency of France, but on 1 January 2002 Euro bank notes and coins will be introduced.

Lanchâtra hamlet squeezes round the path at the entrance to the Vallon de Lanchâtra (Route 55)

Between this date and 30 June 2002 both Euro currency and French francs will be in use, but the franc will cease to exist from 1 July 2002.

Banks are open from 9am until noon, and between 2pm and 4pm Monday (or Tuesday) to Friday, and closed either Saturday or Monday. On the day before a bank holiday, banks usually close early. Most cash machines accept UK bank cash cards.

Banks, post offices and official exchange offices will change foreign currency and travellers cheques. Most major credit cards (Visa, Barclaycard, Carte Bleue, Mastercard/Access, etc) are widely accepted in shops, hotels and restaurants. Should the sign for your own credit card not be on display, check for acceptability before buying.

Health Care

In addition to having insurance cover for accidents, rescue and health care, British nationals (and those of other EU countries) are advised to carry a valid E111 form to obtain free, or reduced-cost, emergency state-provided medical treatment whilst in France. Apply to your local post office for Form E111. Should you fall ill or have an accident during a visit to the Écrins, there are hospitals in Grenoble and Briançon.

Passports and Visas

Nationals of EU countries, including Britain, need only a full, valid passport to visit France – the old British Visitor's Passport is no longer valid here. Visas are not required. Visitors from Australia, Canada and the USA (among others) need a visa only if they plan to stay in France longer than three months.

Post and Telephone Services

Main post offices (La Poste, or PTT) are open from Monday to Friday from 8am to 7pm, and on Saturday mornings from 8am to noon. Smaller branch post offices are often closed at lunchtime between noon and 2pm, and usually close for the day at 4pm. Postage stamps may be bought from newsagents, tobacconists (*tabac*) and shops that sell postcards.

Most public telephone kiosks take phone cards (*télécartes*) which are on sale at post offices, tobacconists and newsagents. *Télécartes* are available in units of 50 or 120. Calls can be received at phone boxes showing a blue bell sign.

The international access code from France is 00. Individual country codes are usually displayed in telephone kiosks. The code for the UK is 44; Eire is 353; the USA is 1.

Finally, all information contained in this guide is given in good faith, and routes described offered in the hope that readers will gain as much enjoyment from walking in and around the Écrins National Park as I have during the weeks of research. But I am fully aware that from time to time changes occur to the landscape, huts, and villages, etc, through natural causes as well as by the hand of man. It may be that you will discover paths that have been rerouted, or landscape features altered to such an extent that some of the descriptions are no longer valid. Should this be the case, I first of all hope that such changes in no way spoil your holiday, and secondly, would very much appreciate a note giving details in order that I can check them out for any future edition of the guide. A postcard sent to me c/o Cicerone Press, 2 Police Square, Milnthorpe, Cumbria LA7 7PY would be gratefully received.

VALLÉE DE LA ROMANCHE

The northern fringe of the Écrins park makes a first-rate introduction to the area. High pasturelands scattered with time-worn hamlets make a perfect belvedere from which to study the glacier-clad bastions of La Meije and Le Râteau, while the abrupt flanks of those mountains are broken here and there with hanging valleys and secretive glens full of raw beauty. Peaceful tarns, anxious rivers and waterfalls add to the valley's charm, and there's no shortage of prime walking potential.

ACCESS AND INFORMATION

Location: On the northern edge of the Écrins National Park. The Romanche flows west from near Col du Lautaret to Bourg d'Oisans, a distance of 57km

Bases: Bourg d'Oisans (720m), La Grave (1481m), Villar d'Arène (1683m)

Information: Office du Tourisme, Quai Girard, 38520 Bourg d'Oisans (☎ 04 76 80 03 25)

Maison du Parc, Rue Gambetta, BP 47, 38520 Bourg d'Oisans (☎ 04 76 80 00 51)

Office du Tourisme, 05320 La Grave (☎ 04 76 79 90 05)

Access: Easily accessible via the N91 Grenoble–Briançon road. Daily bus services operate between Grenoble and Briançon, serving Bourg d'Oisans, La Grave, and points in between

INTRODUCTION

The Romanche is an important valley of access. Rising over 1300m between Bourg d'Oisans and Col du Lautaret, it is flanked by the glacier peaks of La Meije (see Appendix B) and Le Râteau on the south, and high but gently rolling country to the north.

That northern countryside, which is immensely attractive to walkers, is scooped with shallow valleys leading to summits of 3000m and more, while small tarns trapped below reflect the snow and ice of the southern massif. It's a gentle, pastoral landscape, with a handful of small hamlets set upon terraces that face across the valley to its majestic southern wall. La Meije is the highest of those southern mountains, a graceful peak of 3982m and the subject of intense rivalry during attempts to make its first ascent, which was finally achieved in 1877 by Boileau de Castelnau with Pierre Gaspard, father and son. Despite its focus La Meije is just one of several fine peaks near the head of the valley that form an impressive backdrop to a number of walks, while at the western end of its wall the prime ski resort of Les Deux-Alpes laces the hillside with a series of cableways and tows that remain largely unguessed from the valley itself.

From Le Bourg's flat basin ringed with steep crags, the N21 Lautaret–Briançon road travels southeast to enter the Gorges de l'Infernet, then rises steadily to gain some 300m at Lac du Chambon, an emerald green reservoir which flooded three hamlets when its dam was built. At the barrage a minor road (D213) twists south to Mont de Lans and Les Deux-Alpes, while another (D25) climbs north to Mizoën and continues through a deep ravine to Besse, while yet another narrow road aims for the western side of the Plateau d'Emparis. The main N21 skirts the north shore of Lac du Chambon with the aid of tunnels and continues through the narrow Combe de Malaval, which gradually opens until La Grave is reached with its view of La Meije and Le Râteau.

Out of La Grave another minor road (D33) cuts off to the north and twists up the hillside to Ventelon, where it forks. The right-hand option goes to Les Hières and Valfroide, while the left fork eases round to Les Terraces, then climbs on to Le Chazelet. Both roads have tremendous panoramic views to the south.

Meanwhile N21 snakes through more tunnels before emerging

on the edge of Villar d'Arène, the last village on the route to Col du Lautaret, although side roads break off to the hamlets of Le Pied du Col and Les Cours. Col du Lautaret itself offers a striking view of the Mieje massif and its glaciers. At an altitude of 2057m it is said to be the busiest crossing in the Dauphiné Alps, and is kept open throughout the winter. There's a 2 hectare Alpine Garden with over 2000 species of plants, and in the Refuge Napoléon an information centre detailing the geology of the area as well as its flora and fauna. At the col D902 forks north on the way to Col du Galibier (highest crossing on the Route des Grandes Alpes), but N91 continues to the southeast, descending into the Vallée de la Guisane on the way to Briançon.

MAIN VALLEY BASES

* **BOURG D'OISANS** (720m) is one of the main points of entry to the Écrins region, having ready access to both the Romanche and Vénéon valleys and, via Col d'Ornon, to the Valjouffrey. As 'capital' of the region the town has frequent bus connections with Grenoble, and is the terminus for a variety of services, not only through the Romanche but also to La Bérarde, Les Deux-Alpes, Alpe-d'Huez, etc. Le Bourg is situated in an open, sunny basin at the confluence of several valleys. It has a wide assortment of shops, bars and restaurants, a number of hotels, apartments and campsites, three *gîtes d'étape*, a Maison du Parc (national park information office) and a Bureau des Guides. Contact the tourist office for their *Guide des Hébergements* (accommodation list) – address and telephone number at the head of this section. On the hillside more than 1100m above Le Bourg to the northeast lies the ski resort of Alpe d'Huez, reached by a road of numerous hairpins and visited by walkers following GR549, while Bourg d'Oisans marks the starting point for the classic GR54 Tour de l'Oisans.

* **LA GRAVE** (1481m) is situated below La Meije, some 28km from Bourg d'Oisans. While the old village clusters on the steep south-facing hillside, its few shops and hotels mostly line the Lautaret road. There's cableway access to Col des Ruillans

Cascade de la Sarenne on the outskirts of Bourg d'Osians (Route 1)

On the trail to Refuge de l'Alpe de Villar d'Arène (Routes 15, 16, 22)

Refuge de l'Alpe de Villar d'Arène (Routes 15–20)

The Romanche below Refuge de l'Alpe (Route 17)

(3200m) on the edge of the Glacier de la Girose (Téléphérique des Glaciers de la Meije) for all-year skiing and summer tourist visits, and the prospect of lots of good walking nearby. La Grave has five hotels, two *gîtes d'étape* and two campsites; there are several shops and café/restaurants, a tourist office and Bureau des Guides on Place Victor Chaud (☎ 04 76 79 90 21).

• **VILLAR D'ARÈNE** (1683m) is located just off the main road between La Grave and Col du Lautaret, and makes a convenient base for walks in the upper Romanche valley. Facilities include a post office, food stores, bars, five hotels, two *gîtes d'étape* and a campsite (Camping Municipal d'Arsine) at Le Pied du Col, 3km upvalley.

OTHER VALLEY BASES

Travelling upvalley from Le Bourg, rooms are available in **MONT DE LANS** above Lac de Chambon, and at **LE FRENEY D'OISANS** at the western end of the lake. Le Freney also has a campsite (open mid-June to mid-Sept), while nearby **MIZOËN,** on a *variante* of GR54, has a *gîte d'étape* and a two-star hotel. At the small village of **LES FRÉAUX** (1389m), a short distance below La Grave, there's one hotel, a *gîte d'étape* and a campsite. On the steep hillside above the village, the hamlets of **LES TERRACES** and **LE CHAZELET** both have *gîtes* and apartments for rent, while Le Chazelet also has one hotel, Le Relais d'Emparis (one star). On the same hillside **VENTELON** also has a single hotel, La Chaumine, as does **VALFROIDE** (Les 3 Évéchés).

MOUNTAIN HUTS

A number of huts are located on mountains and hillsides within reach of the Vallée de la Romanche. Some are clearly the preserve of climbers, due to their position, although most are accessible to walkers.

• **REFUGE DE L'ALPE DE VILLAR D'ARÈNE** (2079m) is owned by the Briançon section of the CAF (Club Alpin

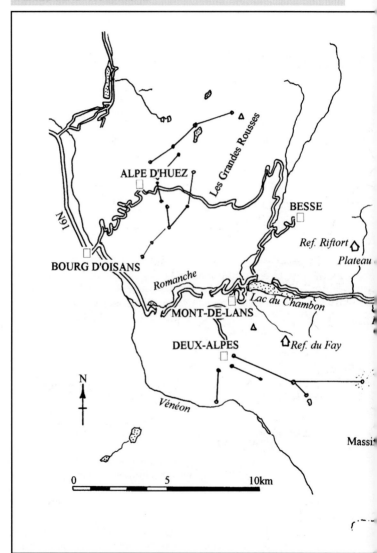

VALLÉE DE LA ROMANCHE

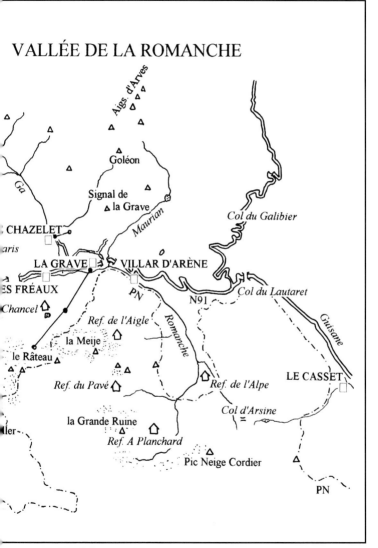

Français). Set among pastures on the route of GR54 near Col d'Arsine, the refuge is manned in springtime and from mid-June to early September, with a full meals service. It has 73 places in summer, 20 in winter, and is reached by a walk of about 2¼hrs from Villar d'Arène (☎ 04 76 79 94 66).

- **REFUGE DU PAVÉ** (2841m) is a small hut with 26 places, also owned by the Briançon section of the CAF. Located by Lac du Pavé at the head of the Cavales valley, about 3½–4hrs walk from Alpe de Villar d'Arène, the hut is manned and with meals provision from the end of June to the beginning of September. For reservations telephone Ref. de l'Alpe de Villar d'Arène.

- **REFUGE ADÈLE PLANCHARD** (3169m) stands high on the Crête de Roche Méane, southwest of Alpe de Villar d'Arène, from which it is gained in 4–4½hrs. Owned by the STD (Societe des Touristes du Dauphiné) the refuge has 64 places and is manned during the high summer, when meals are provided (☎ 04 76 79 92 14).

- **REFUGE DE L'AIGLE** (3450m) is reached by a notoriously steep climb of around 6½hrs, some of the way on a seriously crevassed glacier. Built upon a rock spur dividing the glaciers Tabuchet and de l'Homme on the Meije, this is almost exclusively a climber's hut, but details are given here for interest. Owned by the CAF (Briançon) it can sleep 20, and has a guardian in residence during spring and summer offering a simple meals service (☎ 04 76 79 94 74).

- **REFUGE EVARISTE CHANCEL** (2506m) is privately owned, has 46 places and is manned throughout the year with meals provided. Set on a rocky shelf above Lac du Puy Vachier on the slopes of Le Râteau, the refuge is gained by a walk of 3–3½hrs from La Grave, or about 1hr 15mins from the Gare de Peyrou d'Amont (middle station) of the *téléphérique* (☎ 04 76 79 92 32).

- **REFUGE RIFTORT** (2240m) stands outside the national park on the northern side of the valley near the beautiful Plateau d'Emparis (Plateau de Paris), about 4½hrs walk from Mizoën. Privately owned, it can sleep 40 and is open at weekends from May to mid-June, then permanently until mid-September, followed by weekends only, if reserved in advance, until the end of October. Restaurant service (☎ 04 76 80 24 11).

Route 1: Bourg d'Oisans (720m) – Besse-en-Oisans (1564m) – La Grave (1481m)

Grade:	3
Distance:	34 kilometres
Height gain:	2708 metres
Height loss:	1944 metres
Time:	2 days (total walking time, 15–16hrs)
Accommodation:	*Gîtes d'étape* in Clavans-le-Haut and Besse. Refuge Riftort near the Plateau d'Emparis, *gîtes* and hotel in Le Chazelet, and *gîte* in Les Terraces
Location:	Along the north side of the valley

This reasonably long two-day walk makes a traverse of the north flank of the valley, following GR54 (Tour de l'Oisans) throughout, over country that lies outside the national park boundary. It's a very fine trek, quite demanding in places, always interesting and with some memorably scenic high points.

Leave Bourg d'Oisans by walking along the N21 road in the direction of Briançon. Just after this crosses the Romanche bear left towards Alpe d'Huez. Immediately after passing Camping la Cascade (on the right), and just before the river which comes from the cascade itself, branch right on a footpath which marks the start of GR54. Coming to the waterfall the way veers right and begins to slant up and across a steep rock face using narrow shelves. Red-white paint flashes direct the way and at the top of the slabs you come to a road and the hamlet of La Ville.

Turn right past a large building and cross another road where a path climbs through forest, quite steeply at times. Eventually join a road leading to **Le Châtelard** (*refreshments*), and continue through the hamlet of Maronne to Le Rosay, after which a waymarked path leads across pastureland with views to Huez and Alpe d'Huez, then descends steeply to cross the Sarenne (a gorgeous stream burrowing through a ravine) on a tiny stone bridge, the Pont Romain. Over the bridge the way rises a little then heads to the right on an easy gradient among woods, passing the remains of a mill and another old stone building. Come to a dirt road, and when it forks take the left branch leading all the way to Col de Sarenne (1999m, 5½–6hrs).

On the far side of the pass there's some very wild-looking country with the road snaking across it. Very soon a path descends steeply in tight windings, crosses the road several hundred metres below, then continues as a mule trail to the village of **Clavans-le-Haut** (1396m, 7½hrs: *accommodation, refreshments*).

> *Gîte 'En Cloriette': 15 beds, open all year (☎ 04 76 80 27 03)*

Walk down the road for a further 20mins to reach **Clavans-le-Bas** (1368m, *refreshments*) where the waymarked GR54 descends beside gardens to a bridge over the Ferrand torrent, followed by a tiring uphill climb to **Besse-en-Oisans** (1550m, 9hrs: *accommodation, refreshments*), a charming stone-built village with a food store and two small bars in addition to the hotel and *gîte d'étape*. A campsite is located about 1km further up the road.

> *Hotel Alpin: 7 rooms, open all year (☎ 04 76 80 06 55)*
> *Gîte 'le Sarret': 52 beds in dorms & rooms, open all year (☎ 04 76 80 06 22)*

Beyond Besse the route crosses a stream, slants across the hillside then twists up to Col Nazie (1902m), an easy saddle with a dirt road just below on the south side. Beyond this steepening zigzags bring you to another saddle, Col Bichet (2245m), which is gained a little over 2hrs from Besse. From here you look across an extensive pastureland basin to the Aiguilles de la Saussaz in the northeast, and southeast to the rugged Meije, Le Râteau and their glaciers which form a direct contrast to the gentle foreground.

Note: If you bear left at the col a track leads to Refuge Riftort for accommodation and/or refreshments. 40 places, open weekends May to mid-June, then permanently to mid-Sept, and weekends only to end October (☎ 04 76 80 24 11 or 04 76 80 04 91)

The continuing GR54 crosses the pastureland of the Plateau d'Emparis heading southeast to the junction with GR50, which is also a *variante* of GR54 coming from Mizoën and Lac de Chambon (see Route 3). Beyond this the way rises to Col du Souchet (2365m), then slopes down the other side. (Before long an alternative path diverts to the right in order to visit Lacs Lérié and Noir – recommended; see Routes 3 and 5.) The main trail is clear and obvious as it makes its way across the pastures to a magnificent balcony path with great panoramic views, then on a steep and twisting descent to a bridge over the Torrent du Ga, beyond which lies **Le Chazelet** (1786m, 5hrs from Besse: *accommodation, refreshments*), by far the largest village since leaving Bourg d'Oisans. It has food stores, bars and restaurants, as well as a choice of accommodation.

Hotel le Relais d'Emparis: 14 rooms (☎ 04 76 79 90 10)
Gîte et Refuge Jacquier: 18 places (☎ 04 76 79 95 22)
Auberge Chez Baptiste: 41 places (☎ 04 76 79 92 09)

Leaving the village follow the road as it rises steadily to the much-photographed shrine known as the Oratoire du Chazelet (1840m), which makes an interesting foreground with the Meije soaring across the valley behind it. A few paces beyond the Oratoire take the path which drops to the right and descend to the next village, **Les Terraces** (1782m: *accommodation, refreshments*) about 30mins from Le Chazelet.

Gîte l'Auberge Ensoleillee: 30 places (☎ 04 76 79 95 11)

Pass alongside the church, then follow waymarks round the side of buildings and onto a path that descends through pastures. This leads directly to **La Grave** (1481m: *accommodation, refreshments*), about 6–6½hrs from Besse.

Route 2: Barrage du Chambon (1044m) – Cuculet (1289m) – Mont-de-Lans (1280m) – Barrage du Chambon

Grade:	1
Distance:	6 kilometres
Height gain/loss:	236 metres
Time:	2½–3 hours
Location:	South of Lac du Chambon

This undemanding walk provides views across and along Lac du Chambon, visits a small hamlet and also the village of Mont-de-Lans. Although much of the way is on tracks and minor roads, there should be very little traffic (if any) to contend with.

Leave the *barrage* by walking south along D213 in the direction of Mont-de-Lans, but shortly break off on a track sloping downhill to the left where a sign gives 1hr to Cuculet. Occasional blue waymarks will be seen. Crossing a stream the way turns north, then when it forks you take the upper path which swings uphill heading south. After crossing a meadow enter woodland and, twisting uphill in and out of woods, eventually come to a road leading directly into **Cuculet**. (It's possible to take a path from here down to the lake shore and follow this upvalley to a bridge beyond the lake at 1091m, where you join the main N91 road. Another option is to follow a path climbing southeast to the Refuge de la Fée some 900m or so above the hamlet, reached in about 3hrs from Cuculet.)

The continuing minor road out of Cuculet slopes downhill heading south to cross a stream (Ruisseau de la Pisse) by a bridge at 1247m, then snakes round the hillside to gain **Mont-de-Lans** (*refreshments*). Walk out of the village along D213, which returns to the **Barrage du Chambon**, but note the signed path which breaks off to the right for a short-cut down to the dam. On the way there's a fine view, not only along the lake, but across to Mizoën and its splendid little church.

Route 3: Barrage du Chambon (1044m) – Chalets du Fay (2258m) – Dôme du Lac Noir (2456m)

Grade:	2-3
Distance:	13 kilometres (+ 3km)
Height gain:	1412 metres
Time:	5–5½ hours (+ 45mins)
Accommodation:	Mizoën, and Refuge du Chalet du Fay
Location:	Northeast of Lac du Chambon

The Dôme du Lac Noir is a cairned viewpoint overlooking the Lacs Noir and Lérié on the famed Plateau d'Emparis high on the north bank of the Romanche. It's an understandably popular area, although most visitors either drive part way or walk to it from Le Chazelet, above La Grave. While the amount of height to be gained on the walk described makes it a tough day, the trail, which is a variante of GR54 (as well as being a section of GR50), is mostly straightforward, but with one or two exposed sections. It's recommended to spend a night at the Chalet du Fay gîte, either before or after visiting the lakes. As an alternative to returning to the barrage you could join the main GR54 and continue to La Grave, as outlined in Route 1.

A steep path rises from the Barrage du Chambon to avoid the first two hairpins of the minor road which twists up to **Mizoën** (30mins: *accommodation, refreshments*), a small village at 1186m.

> *Auberge Mizoën: open early May to end October (☎ 04 76 80 19 79)*
> *Le Panoramique: 10 rooms, open except May and Oct–mid Dec*
> *(☎ 04 76 80 06 25)*

In the centre of the village waymarks direct the route between houses, then to the right before rejoining the road very briefly. Take a path on the right once more. This leads to the hamlet of Les Aymes, clustered above the lake, but on leaving you come onto a waymarked path which develops as an exposed trail along the hillside aiming roughly eastward.

Eventually cross a small pasture near Les Clots (1540m, 1¼hrs). Now the way climbs the grassy hillside in zigzags, then crosses above the impressive Cascade de la Pisse and, curving east again, joins a dirt road. Either follow this or the path nearby, which will bring you to the **Refuge du Chalet du Fay** (2258m, 4hrs: *accommodation, refreshments*).

> *Refuge du Chalet du Fay: open June to end Oct (☎ 04 76 80 24 12)*

The way now slopes down a little over pastureland and alongside a stream until coming to a junction (2211m) with the main GR54. Here you turn right and rise easily to gain Col du Souchet (2365m) about 45mins after leaving the Chalet du Fay. Here you'll find another path junction. Bear right and soon reach Lac Noir, a beautiful tarn with reflective views of the Meije and Le Râteau cast in the water. Lac Lérié lies a short distance to the east, sunken slightly in a hollow, while the **Dôme du Lac Noir** is marked by a cairn between the two tarns. The grass hummocks and limestone ribs around the lakes are starred with Alpine plants such as edelweiss, gentians and alpine asters. Other small tarns, pools and dried lakes lie northwest of Lac Noir.

Either return by the way you came (45mins to Chalet du Fay), or retrace your steps to Col du Souchet and there turn right to follow GR54 to Le Chazelet and La Grave (2½–3hrs to La Grave) as described in Route 1.

Route 4: La Grave (1481m) – Les Terraces (1782m) – Le Chazelet (1786m)

Grade:	1–2
Distance:	3 kilometres
Height gain:	375 metres
Height loss:	70 metres
Time:	1hr 15mins
Location:	Northwest of La Grave

Writing of the Meije in 1871, Edward Whymper commented: 'The view of this mountain from the village of La Grave can hardly be spoken of too highly. It is one of the finest road-views in the Alps... But from La Grave one can no more appreciate the noble proportions and the towering height of the Meije, than understand the symmetry of the dome of St Paul's by gazing upon it from the churchyard. To see it fairly, one must be placed at a greater distance and at a greater height.' This walk gives an opportunity to do just that. It climbs the hillside directly above La Grave, visits two of the villages that enjoy a better perspective of La Meije, and provides a good introduction to the area. Although steep in places, it's neither difficult nor too demanding.

Walk up through the old village of La Grave, passing the late 11th-century church on your left and, winding through narrow streets, bear left by the *gîte d'étape* called Le Refuge. At the upper part of the village bear left in front of Le Château. A few paces beyond this a path cuts right to Ventelon – but we go straight ahead on a track signed to Les Terraces (the route of GR54), which can be seen ahead on the steep hillside. The track soon goes through gently-angled meadows, then forks. Take the right-hand option – a path which slants uphill and enters **Les Terraces**. Go ahead between farms and old houses, several of which are adorned with flowers, and come to the church on a road (40mins).

Cross directly ahead, climb a little higher and rejoin the road at a hairpin bend. Walk ahead along the road, but then break away on a track cutting from it at a bend. This short-cuts the road and brings you up to the shrine of Oratoire du Chazelet (1840m) at the road's highest point.

Leave the road for a moment and take the path on the opposite side. This climbs a short distance to an orientation table which provides an extensive panorama dominated by La Meije and Le Râteau. To the northwest lies Le Chazelet. The Romanche is about 500m below, the valley's north wall plunges in crags to the river, while to the east Villar d'Arène can be seen, as can the road snaking up to Col du Lautaret. Along the hillside are clustered several hamlets and farms.

Return to the road and wander down to **Le Chazelet** (1786m: *refreshments*), a crowded village with a medieval atmosphere set just below the confluence of the Torrent du Ga and that of the Martignare.

Route 5: Le Chazelet (1786m) – Plateau
d'Emparis – Lac Noir (2430m)

Grade:	1–2
Distance:	8 kilometres (one way)
Height gain:	644 metres
Time:	2hrs 45mins (4–4½hrs return)
Location:	West of La Grave

This is the third walk to visit the Plateau d'Emparis (marked as Plateau de Paris on the IGN map), and for visitors based at La Grave it is the obvious and more popular route. An elevated pastureland with an atmosphere all its own, the Plateau rewards with tremendous views and an abundance of Alpine plants. If walking all the way from La Grave you should remember to add at least 2½hrs for the return journey. Should you have your own vehicle, there's plenty of parking space on the outskirts of Le Chazelet.

From the parking area on the northwest side of Le Chazelet cross the Torrent du Ga on a bridge where a good path (GR54) then makes a left-hand hairpin and rises steeply with zigzags up the hillside, at first heading southwest. The way then turns to the right, passes beneath a ski-lift and crosses a shoulder at 2164m. This is near the end of the Côte du Caux. Wander round the slopes of the Serre Bernard (a delightful belvedere), cross a stream and slant up to the open, rolling **Plateau d'Emparis**. At about 2300m (2¼hrs) the path forks. Bear left across grass hillocks to find Lac Lérié in its hollow. This is a lovely tarn from whose shores you gaze due south across the unseen depths of the Romanche to the glaciers which adorn the opposite wall, and southeast for a magnificent view of the Meije. Pass round the right-hand side of the tarn and wander west over more hummocks to the larger **Lac Noir**.

To return to Le Chazelet, follow the minor path heading roughly north, then northeast to Col du Souchet, where you come onto the GR54. Bear right and follow this all the way back to the car park.

Other Walks from Le Chazelet

- A short and easy round trip of about 50mins leads to the small Alp hut of **LES PLAGNES** in the lower reaches of the Combe de Martignare, northeast of Le Chazelet. The Combe is a pastoral glen rimmed by grass-covered mountains, and the path to take is that which forks by a white ski-school building above the road at a hairpin bend northwest of the village.

- A second option is to take the path along the east bank of the Torrent du Ga to the hamlets of **RIVET DU PIED**, **RIVET DU MILIEU** and **RIVET DE LA CIME**, and continue as far as you like towards the head of the glen which narrows below Pic du Mas de la Grave.

- The ascent of **PIC DU MAS DE LA GRAVE** (3020m) makes a straightforward but rewarding day out from Le Chazelet (5hrs ascent, 8hrs there and back). For this, take the path mentioned above through Rivet du Pied, etc, as far as the Baraque de la Buffe (1¾hrs, 2085m), where several streams come together to create the Torrent du Ga. The way then climbs southwest, before flanking north-northwest above a hanging valley. Cairns mark the start of the ascent proper which strikes up the mountain's grassy southwest ridge. This turns to rock at about 2650m, and more cairns guide the way to the summit. Views from here are extensive.

- A two-day circular walk, with a night spent at **REFUGE RIFTORT** (see Route 1), follows the path mentioned above through the Vallon de la Ga as far as the Baraque de la Buffe, then curves southwest to cross a grassy spur at about 2275m. Over this wander alongside the Rif Tort stream which brings you close to the refuge. On the second day cross the pastureland of the Plateau d'Emparis to join GR54, and take this path heading southeast over Col du Souchet and down to Le Chazelet.

Route 6: La Grave (1481m) – Oratoire du Chazelet (1840m) – Signal de la Grave (2446m) – Ventelon (1755m) – La Grave

Grade:	2–3
Distance:	13 kilometres
Height gain/loss:	965 metres
Time:	5–5½hrs
Location:	North of La Grave

A fairly long and demanding, but by no means difficult, route to a modest summit viewpoint north of La Grave, this outing needs settled weather to gain maximum enjoyment from it. A wonderful overview of the region is gained from many parts of the walk, but the descent to Ventelon is very steep in places and can be rather tiring.

Follow directions to the orientation table above the Oratoire du Chazelet, as outlined in Route 4. At an altitude of 1856m, this is gained in about an hour from La Grave. Continue on the path above the orientation table (direction Les Clots and Signal de la Grave), angling gently up through meadows with good views onto Le Chazelet. About 10mins from the road you will come to a junction marked by a signpost. The right-hand path goes to Les Clots, but we take the alternative which makes a rising traverse of the left-hand hillside.

Approaching a chairlift views open to reveal the Vallon de la Ga topped by Pic du Mas de la Grave. Beyond the chairlift the way curves right into the Combe de Martignare, banked with wild flowers. The track is joined by another shortly after reaching a ski tow, and on passing under the tow the way cuts back on itself in a hairpin. When the track forks soon after, take the left branch to pass under the ski tow once more. The way snakes uphill virtually following the line of another ski tow, and emerges onto a grass saddle at its head (2hrs).

Bear left at the saddle and rise up the broad but steeply sloping grass ridge to gain a domed high point of 2271m. Beyond this descend to a second saddle (2252m) where a grass path cuts back to the right – this is used on the descent to Ventelon. Ignore this alternative for now and continue along the ridge, with **Signal de la Grave** and its summit cairn seen ahead. The path rises to it without complication, reaching the crown with its impressive panoramic views about 2hrs 45mins from La Grave.

Descend by the same path as far as the second saddle (2252m) met on the ascent, then slant downhill slightly left ahead – now aiming south. It's a grass path which becomes intermittent, but with a few tiny cairns to direct the way. Soon Les Terraces is seen directly ahead, then you suddenly discover Les Clots lying below. After angling across the hillside the way then descends very steeply to join the path linking Les Clots with the saddle at the head of the ski tow. Turn left and at the next junction bear right.

Coming to Les Clots join a track which swings left then right and curves round the hillside to bring you into **Ventelon** (1755m, 4hrs: *refreshments*). Bear right along the main street to pass below the hotel/bar, and wander along the road which leads to Les Terraces. When you reach the church (20mins from Ventelon) bear left and descend to **La Grave** via the waymarked GR54 by which the walk began.

> *Note: To make a 1¾hr circular walk from the Oratoire, bear right at the first saddle and go down to its lowest part, then left on a descending path to Les Clots. From that hamlet take another signed path which angles across the hillside roughly westward, and brings you to the path junction above the orientation table. Go down to the road.*

Route 7: La Grave (1481m) – Hameau de Valfroide (1874m) – Lac du Goléon (2438m)

Grade:	2
Distance:	7 kilometres (one way)
Height gain:	957 metres
Time:	3–3½hrs (5½hrs return)
Location:	Northeast of La Grave

Lac du Goléon lies trapped by a glacial sill at the lower end of a hanging valley northeast of La Grave. The walk to it from the string of hamlets that make up the Hameau de Valfroide is a popular one in the high summer season, but that is understandable for it's an interesting route, not too demanding, and with some very fine views to enjoy. Visitors with their own transport could drive as far as Les Hières and walk from there, thus saving about an hour on the initial section, although the walk from La Grave itself encourages a leisurely study of the balcony villages and hamlets that enjoy such splendid outlooks to the Meije.

Walk uphill through La Grave, passing the church to your left, and make for the highest part of the village where you bear left in front of Le Château. A few paces later break away on a path on the right signed to Ventelon. It's a clear path which climbs steeply through flower-filled meadows – often with views onto the rooftops of La Grave – and eventually comes out onto a road after about 35mins. Cross straight ahead to short-cut a hairpin, rejoining the road moments later. Walk towards Ventelon, seen just above, but take the right branch at a junction on the D333, direction Les Hières.

From the road the Meije looks very fine, its full stature more clearly appreciated than from La Grave. As the road curves, Les Hières can be seen ahead, with the Vallée du Maurian behind it. About 1km from Ventelon come to the entrance to **Les Hières** (1770m, 55mins: *refreshments*) where the road forks. Remain on the upper road through the village which, like so many in the neighbourhood, consists of stone-built houses with grey corrugated roofs.

On the eastern side of Les Hières the road becomes a stony track edging into the narrow glen of the Maurian torrent, at the head of which can be seen the obvious glacial sill behind which lies Lac du Goléon.

The way leads through the small hamlets that come under the general heading of the **Hameau de Valfroide**. Some of the buildings are old and dilapidated, but others have been renovated as holiday homes. The first group is known as **Petit Pramailler** (1hr 20mins); the next is **Pramailler** (*refreshments*), about 3mins beyond the first and with a hotel (Refuge Les 3 Eveches). A path breaks away left here to a higher hamlet, La Sauce, but we continue to a third hamlet, **Le Pré Rond**. Just after crossing a stream by two houses, note the bridge on the right which takes a path to Lac du Pontent and Villar d'Arène (Route 8), as well as offering an alternative descent to La Grave via Le Puy Golèfre.

Remain on the track heading deeper into the valley and come to **Le Plot**, where the track ends. A footpath continues through pastures and on to a more stony landscape. Towards the head of the glen it twists uphill in numerous zigzags and eventually tops a high point over which lies a plateau of pastureland. Slope gently down to the shores of **Lac du Goléon** (3hrs from La Grave), and from the far northern end, where the shoreline is fluffed with cotton grass, a view back shows the distant Meije and Le Râteau once more.

To return to La Grave reverse the upward route, allowing about 2hrs.

Note: *A trail pushes on into the upper reaches of the Vallée du Maurian which is guarded by the Aiguille du Goléon, Aiguilles de la Saussaz and Aiguille d'Agentière. The apex of the linking ridges forms the Aiguilles d'Arves which run in a line away from the Maurian and defeated Whymper's party when he came here in 1864. About 30mins from the lake a small, locked and windowless hut has been built against a large boulder, the so-called Refuge Carraud. Beyond it the trail progresses towards the head of the glen, then forks. The ascent of the 3427m Aiguille du Goléon branches left (3hrs from the refuge – rope, ice-axe and crampons needed), while the other option climbs to the Col des Trois Pointes (3043m).*

Route 8: La Grave (1481m) – Hameau de Valfroide (1874m) – Lac du Pontet (1982m) – Villar d'Arène (1683m) – La Grave

Grade:	2–3
Distance:	14 kilometres
Height gain/loss:	784 metres
Time:	5½–6hrs
Location:	Northeast and east of La Grave

The pretty Lac du Pontet lies in a pastoral bowl 300m above Villar d'Arène, but could easily be reached by visitors with their own transport by a walk of just 20mins. However, the route described here makes a full-day's outing with lots of interest throughout. It begins with a steep climb to the villages and hamlets that line the upper hillside above La Grave, then mounts a steep grass slope below l'Aiguillon (an excellent viewpoint) before dropping to the farm of Le Chazelet just below the lake. After visiting the lake descent is made to Villar d'Arène, followed by an undulating walk back to La Grave on the south bank of the Romanche. A fairly long walk, but without difficulty.

Follow directions given under Route 7 as far as **Le Pré Rond** (1½hrs), then bear right to cross the footbridge over the Maurian torrent. The subsequent path goes downstream a short distance, and about 2mins from the bridge it forks. The branch that goes straight ahead leads to Le Puy Golèfre and La Grave, but we take the left branch slanting up the flower-rich hillside, at first gently, then quite steeply, but easing once more on a high sloping meadowland with superb views. The dominant flowers here are the tall yellow gentian (*Gentiana lutea*), harebells and the martagon lily.

About 45mins from the bridge come onto the broad, grass-covered Col de l'Aiguillon (2059m) below the domed Aiguillon summit (2095m) – 10mins to the top for an excellent overview of the valley and a full-frontal view of La Meije; a bench seat allows you to contemplate this in comfort. Return to the col and take the path (almost a track) which angles down the eastern side and becomes a more profound track as height is lost. At the foot of the initial slope the track makes an easy but slightly descending contour (delightful walking), with the Lautaret road seen snaking in the distance and the upper reaches of the Vallée de la Romanche to the right of that.

Eventually come to a parking area on an access road (3hrs) and turn left. Rounding the first hairpin use a path on the left to short-cut the next, then keep on the road until it ends just above a single farm building. A track then strikes ahead over rolling pastures, and 10mins from the roadhead brings you to the little **Lac du Pontet** (3½hrs). A refreshment kiosk is found just above the southwest shore.

Go down the road and descend to **Les Cours** (1779m) using a variety of footpath short-cuts. On reaching the first building of the village take a path cutting sharply to the right and signed to Villar d'Arène. This takes you past a small chapel and down to the main road on the edge of **Villar d'Arène** (1683m, 4¼hrs: *refreshments*). Wander down to the village square and, facing the church, turn sharp left to pass by Auberge Aux 3 Frênes. A red-white waymark directs you onto a path which slopes down to the river and crosses by footbridge. Go through a gate and enter the Parc National des Écrins, and take the right branch where the path forks. This climbs through larchwoods to cross a high spur of land at about 1740m, then descends steeply to a crossing track. Turn right and follow this down to a minor road opposite Camping de la Meije, then bear right again, soon to cross a bridge over the Romanche. The road now slants uphill into **La Grave**.

Route 9: La Grave (1481m) – Les Fréaux (1389m) – La Grave

Grade:	1
Distance:	5½ kilometres
Height gain/loss:	120 metres
Time:	1hr 45mins
Location:	West of La Grave

This pleasant walk is recommended for a summer's evening. It makes for a gentle stroll, initially along the south bank of the Romanche, then returns to La Grave through meadows above the road. Refreshments are available in Les Fréaux.

The walk begins at the eastern (uphill) end of La Grave's main street opposite Hotel Le Serac, where a minor road slopes downhill to Camping de la Meije. At the foot of the slope, where it forks, cross the Romanche and enter the national park. The road swings to the right and keeps company with the river – at first there are steep meadows rising above trees on the left, while across the river both La Grave and Les Terraces can be seen. The road is soon flanked by trees on both sides, but when these give way note a stone-built, hump-backed bridge spanning the river. Immediately after this cross a glacial torrent pouring from the Meije (a path cuts left here to Ref. Chancel, etc) and continue down the road. Soon you'll see a wooden bridge across the river offering access to La Grave.

Passing beneath the *téléphérique* cross a second glacial torrent and immediately turn right onto a narrow footpath which goes alongside the Romanche. This provides a very pleasant walk among pine, larch, silver birch, rowan, alder and wild roses.The path becomes a track, continues among larch trees, then curves up to the road again by an open meadow. Before long note the fine cascade showering down the crags on the right-hand side of the valley – this drains the Torrent du Ga which forms above Le Chazelet.

The road now slopes gently downhill, then curves right to cross the river (45–60mins). Over the Romanche a track breaks away to the right for the return to La Grave, but if you want refreshment wander up into **Les Fréaux** (note the small chapel with mill wheel fitted to the roadside wall), where there's the hotel/bar/restaurant Les Relais des Campeurs beside the main road.

To return to **La Grave** take the track noted above. In a few paces it forks. Ignore the left-hand option and keep ahead to pass between houses, then slant up to the main valley road. Cross to a continuing path/farm track which rises between trees and through meadows, soon with La Grave in view ahead. Just beyond the entrance to Camping Le Gravelotte come onto the road and walk on into the village.

Route 10: La Grave (1481m) – Lac de Puy Vachier (2382m) – Refuge Evariste Chancel (2506m)

Grade:	2–3
Distance:	5 kilometres (one way)
Height gain:	1025 metres
Time:	3–3½hrs
Location:	Southwest of La Grave

Lodged in a glacial cirque bounded by dark crags, the little Lac de Puy Vachier is situated high on the north flank of Le Râteau, while about 30mins above its northwest rim sits the Refuge Evariste Chancel. This modest, privately-owned hut was built in 1894, the cost of construction being partly met by the wife of the Hautes-Alpes Deputé. The route to it is steep in places, but recommended for fit walkers, although a much shorter approach is possible from the middle station of the téléphérique (see Route 11).

Begin in the *téléphérique* car park at the western end of La Grave's main street. Just left of the *téléphérique* building a narrow, unmarked path slants downhill among trees to the Romanche, which it crosses by a wooden bridge. Coming to a minor road bear left and about 300m later take a broad signed path on the right. Rising at an easy angle at first, the path then steepens before contouring with a view across the valley to La Grave. The way brings you to the mouth of a ravine drained by the Torrent de la Béous, where there's a junction. Ignore the left branch and continue ahead, descending to cross the torrent then sneaking into the ravine where the path becomes more narrow. It twists uphill and crosses an open meadow with a view of hanging glaciers and a hint of one of the Puy Vachier chalets.

Continuing to climb (sometimes steeply), the path goes among larchwoods and over meadows, always left of the cableway. About 1hr 10mins from La Grave come to a junction of paths at 1882m – the Chalet de Puy Vachier is just off to the left.

> *Note: The left-hand path goes to the Chalet de Chal Vachère and is used on the circular walk described as Route 13.*

Continue uphill, but after a few metres contour to the right and soon pass beneath the *téléphérique*, beyond which you wander through the open larchwoods of the Bois des Fréaux. Coming to another path junction by a large boulder known as the Pierre Farabo (2073m, 1hr 45mins), turn left, still climbing. (The right-hand trail descends steeply to Les Fréaux.) Before long emerge from the woods to the steep pastures of Côte Fine, where the gradient is more severe than hitherto and the path has several braidings – Ref. Chancel can be seen high above, perched on a line of crags.

Reach the upper limit of the Côte Fine pastures in about 2hrs 15mins to find another path junction. The left-hand option here makes a traverse to the Gare de Peyrou d'Amont, but we bear right and progress up a more stony landscape, and about 10mins later arrive at the northeast outflow of **Lac de Puy Vachier** (2382m, 2hrs 25mins). The almost circular, inky-blue tarn is backed by screes and soaring cliffs which curve around it in a tight glacial cirque. The western slope is more broken, and it is on this that the hut is set. The path winds up to the right in undemanding fashion and gains **Refuge Evariste Chancel** (2506m: *accommodation, refreshments*) about 30mins from the lake. The summit of La Meije can be seen from here, as can the Plateau d'Emparis on the far side of the valley. Descent by the same path will take about 2–2½hrs. As an alternative, follow directions for Route 12 which makes a longer, but more interesting, descent to La Grave.

> **Note:** *Perhaps the most challenging walk (Grade 3) from the refuge is that which climbs above the hut, ascending steeply over rough terrain to gain the 2836m Brèche de Paccave (1½hrs) almost due south of the refuge. From here the spires of La Meije look stunning. On the east side of the brèche a vague trail descends steeply, then eases over rocks and boulders, crosses a stream and sharp moraine wall and goes down through the Vallons de la Meije to join a path near the Chalet de Chal Vachère described in Route 12. A strenuous route of 4–4½hrs.*

Route 11: Gare de Peyrou d'Amont (2416m) – Lac de Puy Vachier (2382m)

Grade:	**2**
Distance:	**1½ kilometres**
Height loss:	**34 metres**
Time:	**45mins**
Location:	**Middle station of the Téléphérique des Glaciers de la Meije, southwest of La Grave**

The Téléphérique des Glaciers de la Meije rises in two sections: the first as far as the rock rib of Peyrou d'Amont, the second to Col des Ruillans (3200m) on the northwest slopes of Le Râteau, with spectacular views throughout. (The téléphérique operates in summer from late June to early

September.) From the upper station visitors flock to a commercialised ice grotto, or enjoy huge panoramic views that include the Aiguilles d'Arves, Mont Thabor and, far off, Mont Blanc. The middle station provides better views of La Meije. It offers a short, if rough, walk to the Lac de Puy Vachier and Refuge Chancel, and also gives access to the so-called Vallons de la Meije.

Descend a short distance from the Gare de Peyrou d'Amont (middle station) to a signed path junction virtually beneath the cableway and turn left. This trail descends rough ground, then makes a long undulating traverse of mountainside heading west. In places the path is very thin, but paint flashes act as waymarks. There are several rock tips to negotiate, and in poor visibility the route may not be easy to follow – concentration is called for at all times.

Eventually come to a junction at the head of a steep sloping pasture – the right-hand path here descends to La Grave. Continue, now veering slightly left and rising to **Lac de Puy Vachier**, about 10mins above the junction. Note that the **Refuge Evariste Chancel** can be seen above the lake to the west. To gain the hut allow an extra 30mins – refreshments available.

Either return to the *téléphérique* by the same path, or descend to La Grave via the Chalet de Puy Vachier as signposted (and described in reverse as Route 10) – a steep path taking about 1½hrs from the lake.

Route 12: Refuge Evariste Chancel (2506m) – Gare de Peyrou d'Amont (2416m) – Chal Vachère (1844m) – La Grave (1481m)

Grade:	2
Distance:	7 kilometres
Height loss:	1025 metres
Time:	3hrs
Location:	Southwest and south of La Grave

A varied, scenic descent over mixed terrain, with excellent views to the North Face of the Meije and the turmoil of its glaciers. This is a recommended alternative way down to La Grave from the Chancel refuge.

From the refuge descend to Lac de Puy Vachier and continue to the path junction at the head of the Côte Fine pastures. Veer right to contour the steep hillside heading northeast towards the **Gare de Peyrou d'Amont** (middle station of the *téléphérique*). This section reverses Route 11 above. The way is rough underfoot and with an assortment of rock tips that obscure the path, although waymarks help. As a *téléphérique* pylon comes in view the trail rises and, just below the middle station, reaches a signed junction (45mins–1hr).

Turn left to descend, and about 5mins later you will reach a second junction, where you turn right. (The alternative path descends directly to the Chalets de Puy Vachier.) The way now is a fine path which soon rewards with a lovely view to the hanging Glacier du Râteau. Though narrow, the trail is clear and with large cairns that lead down to larchwoods, with almost constant glacier views.

Having descended among trees for a short distance you emerge to a grass promontory that makes a belvedere from which to study the hanging glacier. Continue down among larchwoods again and come to another junction. (The right-hand path leads into the Vallon de la Meije.) Take the left path, soon twisting steeply downhill and coming to masses of wild raspberries. At the next path junction (still in the woods) take the right-hand option in the direction of Chal Vachère. This contours, then emerges to yet another fine glacier view.

Descend a brief rock tip, go through a few more larches, and come to the Torrent de la Béous which you cross on a wooden footbridge – this is a splendid place of wild streams and glaciers. Over the torrent bear left and wander down through pastures, crossing several minor streams, and come to the solitary **Chalet de Chal Vachère** (1844m, 1hr 45mins). The pastures here are rich in wild flowers and backed by the soaring, glacier-hung North Face of La Meije. Across the valley to the north the string of villages and hamlets can be seen high above La Grave, while near at hand the Béous torrent has carved a narrow ravine below to the left.

Below Chal Vachère the path is funnelled through a steep trough with La Grave in view. As the trough eases, the path progresses to a view of two of the Puy Vachiere chalets on the left bank of the torrent. Come onto a broad path and veer right along the head of pastures, with La Grave seen on the far side of the valley, and descend to a minor road where you bear left. After about 300m turn right on a track to cross the Romanche on a wooden bridge. Bear right, then left up a slope to come onto the *téléphérique* car park on the edge of **La Grave**.

Route 13: La Grave (1481m) – Puy Vachier (1882m) – Chal Vachère (1844m) – La Grave

Grade:	2
Distance:	5 kilometres
Height gain/loss:	401 metres
Time:	2¼–2½hrs
Location:	South of La Grave

This circular walk across the lower slopes of Le Râteau and the Meije links sections of Routes 10 and 12 through woodland and across sloping pastures with plenty of visual highlights.

The walk begins in the car park of the Téléphérique des Glaciers de la Meije and descends an unmarked path found a little left of the *téléphérique* building. Cross the Romanche on a wooden bridge and bear left along a minor road for about 300m. On coming to a broad signed path on the right (direction Refuge Evariste Chancel), leave the road and follow this path as it slopes gently uphill, then more steeply, before making a contour to the right. A fine view shows La Grave across the valley.

At the mouth of a ravine keep ahead at a path junction (the return path emerges at this point). The way crosses the Torrent de la Béous then goes into the ravine, where the path can be rather muddy at times. Twisting uphill you emerge from the ravine and cross an open meadow to gain a view of hanging glaciers high above. The trail climbs on, keeping well to the left of the *téléphérique*, and about 1hr 10mins from La Grave brings you to another path junction at 1882m.

Bear left, passing the upper **Chalet de Puy Vachier**, and wander through larchwoods heading roughly southeast. When the path forks soon after, with one climbing to the right, ignore this and continue on the lower option (direction Chal Vachère). Still in the larchwoods the way contours among wild raspberries, then the woods open to afford a lovely view of the Glacier du Râteau. Descend over rocks, pass through a belt of larches, and come to the wild Torrent de la Béous, from whose bank you gain spectacular views of glaciers, rock walls and screes.

Cross by a footbridge and descend through rough pastures where you will find the **Chalet de Chal Vachère** (1844m). Continue downhill to descend a steep trough to the right of the Béous ravine, and when you reach a broad crossing path turn right. This path was followed near the beginning of the walk, and it leads to the minor road on the south bank of the Romanche. Turn left on the road and about 300m later cross a bridge over the river, then walk up the slope to the *téléphérique* car park.

Route 14: La Grave (1481m) – Villar d'Arène (1683m) – La Grave

Grade:	1–2
Distance:	6 kilometres
Height gain/loss:	332 metres
Time:	2hrs
Location:	East of La Grave

This circular outing links the two neighbouring villages, mostly along the south bank of the Romanche. On the outward walk the route keeps close to the river before crossing and climbing an exposed trail above a series of cataracts, then provides a walk into Villar d'Arène by a roadside meadow and a track. The return uses an undulating route (GR54) through woodland and over a spur of high land. Villar d'Arène has some attractive side streets and opportunities for refreshment.

At the eastern end of La Grave, opposite Hotel Le Serac, go down a slip road leading to Camping de la Meije, but when it curves right at the foot of the slope go ahead over a bridge and immediately turn left. A footpath now goes into trees and shortly forks. Keep ahead on the left branch which follows the river. In and out of patches of woodland the path gradually gains height and enters the river gorge, where the Romanche can be heard thundering over rocks below. After a while the trail ascends a few steps, then descends to river level and crosses to the north bank on a footbridge deep within the gorge.

Making a couple of twists, the trail then angles across the steep flank to gain what is little more than a ledge of a path carved from the gorge wall. From this you gaze down to where the Romanche pours over a series of cataracts. At the end of the 'ledge' section you go through trees and come to a fork just below where the road emerges from a tunnel. Turn right and cut across a small meadow into trees again. The way may be wet and muddy here, but you soon come out into the open and angle up a sloping meadow, from where you can look back to Les Terraces and Ventelon on the hillside above unseen La Grave.

At the top of the meadow skirt the road for about 100m, then go directly ahead on a track which brings you alongside a cemetery with **Villar d'Arène** (*refreshments*) just ahead. Pass to the right of the church and into the *place*, the village square (1hr).

To return to La Grave leave the square at its right-hand corner beside the Auberge Aux 3 Frênes, where a red-white waymark directs you onto a path that descends to a footbridge over the river. Across this enter the national park and bear right on a trail which rises through larchwoods to cross a high spur of land at about 1740m. You then descend to a crossing track, turn right and wander down to a minor road opposite Camping de la Meije. Bear right. The road soon crosses the Romanche and slants uphill to emerge on the main road near the Hotel Le Serac on the edge of **La Grave**.

Other Walks from La Grave

• A multi-day circuit of the **AIGUILLES D'ARVES** could be made by experienced mountain trekkers in the country north of La Grave. This could be achieved by going up to Le Chazelet and pushing through the Combe de Martignare, where the 2763m Col de Martignare is crossed at its head. On the far side an awkward route flanks the west side of the Aiguilles d'Arve to reach a *gîte d'étape* at Le Peron. From there next day cross Col de l'Epaisseur (2891m), northeast of the Aiguilles, and descend to Refuge des Aiguilles d'Arve or to Bonnenuit in the valley below. A return to La Grave is made via the Combe de Mortavieille and Col du Goléon (2873m), followed by an easy trek through the Vallée du Maurian and Hameau de Valfroide.

- A number of *via ferratae* have been established in the Écrins region, one of which tackles the steep north wall of the valley below Les Fréaux near Le Grand Clot. The **VIA FERRATA DE LA GRAVE** has an added interest in that it is situated near the site of the ancient Mines du Grand Clot. The route, like all such 'climbing trails', is equipped with cables, etc, but should only be attempted by activists using the standard safety precautions. (The Bureau des Guides at La Grave organise ascents: ☎ 04 76 79 90 21.) From the foot of the crags to the Plateau d'Emparis, the climb is about 700m high, is equipped with 2000m of cable, and takes 3–4hrs, followed by a walk of about 1½–2hrs down to La Grave.

Route 15: Villar d'Arène (1683m) – Refuge de l'Alpe de Villar d'Arène (2079m)

Grade:	2
Distance:	7 kilometres (one way)
Height gain:	396 metres
Time:	2hrs 15mins (4hrs round trip)
Location:	Southeast of Villar d'Arène

Refuge de l'Alpe de Villar d'Arène is understandably popular, although the majority of its visitors do not stay overnight, but use its facilities on their way to or from a more remote mountain destination. Set on a broad grassy shelf, the hut enjoys an impressive outlook to big peaks (La Grande Ruine in particular) crowding the head of the Vallée de la Romanche to the southwest. A shorter approach to the Refuge de l'Alpe is given as Route 16.

From the village square in Villar d'Aréne, beside Auberge Aux 3 Frênes, take the waymarked path beside gardens and down to the Romanche. Cross by footbridge and bear left. The path rises among trees, then continues as an undulating trail among larches with the milky glacial river below. It then slopes down to river level and passes through an enchanting region of silver birch and larch, rosebay willowherb and beautifully trim, lawn-like grass areas, while the river chunters over gravel beds.

About 40mins from Villar d'Arène come onto a road and bear left. (Immediately on the right here a path cuts off to Ref. de l'Aigle in 6½hrs.) Cross the river and, a few paces later, turn right at a crossing road. Just above can be seen the hamlet of Le Pied du Col. Keep on the road, and 5mins later pass a campsite on the left and, on the right, **Refuge du Pas de l'Ane** (*refreshments*), a *gîte* often used by trekkers tackling the Tour de l'Oisans.

Just beyond the *gîte* the road crosses a bridge and comes to a parking area. The path (GR54) cuts along the lower slopes of the left-hand hillside and later joins a broad path coming from the last parking area, where a sign gives 1hr 15mins to the refuge. Shortly before the way begins to rise, note the view to the right where you look briefly at Pic Gaspard and La Meije.

The way now twists up into a narrow fold of mountainside with the river thundering through a rocky defile to the south. Cross a footbridge and gain height in zigzags, noting the cascades that pour over a cliff above to the left. On topping a bluff come to a junction of paths. The right-hand trail goes to the Sources de la Romanche (Route 17) and the Planchard and Pavé refuges, but we go left (direction Ref. de l'Alpe and Col d'Arsine). Continue in long zigzags to reach a high and almost level pastureland. Wandering across this you come to a junction with the trail from Col du Lautaret (Route 16). Keep ahead and soon the hut will be seen ahead. At the next fork in the path veer half-right to reach the **Refuge de l'Alpe de Villar d'Arène** (*refreshments*), a comfortable and idyllically placed hut.

Allow 1½–2hrs for a return to Villar d'Arène by the same path.

Route 16: Col du Lautaret (2057m) – Refuge de l'Alpe de Villar d'Arène (2079m)

Grade:	2
Distance:	6 kilometres (one way)
Height gain:	22 metres
Time:	1hr 45mins
Location:	East of Villar d'Arène

The Sentier des Crevasses is not what it seems. This is a standard mountain path that goes nowhere near a crevassed glacier, but makes a short and very scenic approach to the Alpe refuge, with a narrow, exposed section where care needs to be taken. It begins just below the Col du Lautaret, and joins the GR54 (Route 15) in the pastureland a short distance north of the hut. For walkers with their own transport, there's plenty of parking space at the col. The Bourg d'Oisans to Briançon bus via La Grave and Villar d'Arène also stops at the col. Views of La Meije are magnificent from the Lautaret, and also from the Sentier.

From Col du Lautaret walk back down the road towards Villar d'Arène, and just after rounding the first sharp bend note the signpost on the left directing the start of the trail to Refuge de l'Alpe and Col d'Arsine. Passing beneath a power line the trail parallels the road for a short distance along the edge of the Réserve Naturelle de Combeynot, then curves south as the Sentier des Crevasses, an exposed and in places rather narrow path with fixed cable for safety. At the end of this section the trail slopes down into pastureland to join the main GR54 at a signed junction. Continue heading south with the hut coming into view, and veer right at the next junction in order to reach the **Refuge de l'Alpe de Villar d'Arène** (2079m: *accommodation, refreshments*). (The left-hand path goes to Col d'Arsine.)

Route 17: Villar d'Arène (1683m) – Sources de la Romanche (2150m)

Grade:	1–2
Distance:	10 kilometres (one way)
Height gain:	467 metres
Time:	3hrs 15mins (5½hrs round trip)
Location:	Southeast of Villar d'Arène

A truly splendid walk in magnificent surroundings, this fairly undemanding route leads to the headwaters of the Romanche below the Glacier de la Plate des Agneaux in a hidden glen walled by La Grande Ruine (3765m) and Pic d'Arsine (3272m), and with Roche Faurio (3730m) forming the southern headwall. But before you are drawn into that upper glen, the walk takes you through a delight of mountain scenery sufficient in itself to make this a very worthwhile outing.

Follow directions for Route 15 as far as the footbridge over a sidestream near a rocky defile about 1½hrs from Villar d'Arène. Cross the footbridge and climb the zigzags from which you can see cascades pouring over a cliff above to the left. Topping a bluff the path forks (1845m). The left-hand option is the direct route to Refuge de l'Alpe and Col d'Arsine, but we take the right-hand alternative, where the path works its way round and over minor slabs (at one point aided by wooden steps) eventually to emerge into a beautiful valley whose pastures are sliced by the Romanche, and which has the block of Montagne des Agneaux and Pic de Neige Cordier forming a wall some way ahead.

The way strikes through the valley keeping left of the stream. As you progress, Roche Faurio and its glacial scarves come into view. Where the valley curves to the right at the Plan de l'Alpe, note a trig point on a grass saddle above left – this is by the unseen Refuge de l'Alpe. Come to a sidestream and a path junction on the bend of the valley; the unmarked left-hand trail leads in 10mins up to the refuge (*refreshments*), but we cross the sidestream veering right and remain along the left-hand side of the Romanche, with La Grande Ruine seen ahead where it subdivides the valley.

The stream is crystal clear as it hastens downvalley, and in one place has formed a little green tarn. Above this, where the valley forks in the Plan de Valfourche, a footbridge crosses the Romanche (2048m, 2hrs 45mins) with a sign giving 2½hrs to Refuge Pavé by the right-hand path. The route to the Sources de la Romanche does not cross the bridge, however, and the signpost here suggests 30mins to the Source and, perhaps optimistically, 3hrs to Refuge Planchard.

Roche Faurio's great headwall is truly impressive now, like something transported from Chamonix, and the way towards it only enhances that impression. The path rounds a boulder spur (a notable spot for marmots) and the valley ahead becomes much less serene than before, littered as it is with rocks and boulders, while Roche Faurio dominates every step of the way through.

Go up a rise and reach a tiny meadowland. Just beyond that, at around 2150m, the **Romanche** emerges in several places from a huge rock tip and heaps of old moraine. Above this point the valley is filled with mountain débris to create a very austere scene.

Either return to Villar d'Arène by the same route, or cut up to the Refuge de l'Alp and follow the main GR54 path back downvalley.

Note: To visit the Sources de la Romanche from the Refuge de l'Alpe simply take the path which descends to the pastures of Plan de l'Alpe below to the south, and follow the trail described above along the left-hand side of the Romanche. Allow 1hr 15mins there, plus about 45mins back to the hut.

Route 18: Refuge de l'Alpe (2079m) – Refuge Adèle Planchard (3169m)

Grade:	3
Distance:	7 kilometres (one way)
Height gain:	1174 metres
Time:	4–4½hrs
Location:	Southwest of Refuge de l'Alpe

The first part of this hut approach is the same as the walk to the Sources de la Romanche (Route 17), but above that the way climbs very steeply up the rocky east flank of the Roche Méane.

Vallée de la Guisane, from the route to Col de l'Eychauda (Route 24)

West of Ailefroide, the Vallon de la Sélé is the setting for Routes 33–35

From Vallon de Clapouse, looking north to Mont Pelvoux (Routes 27, 33)

The wild Vallon de Clapouse, setting for the challenging Route 27

The approach to Refuge Sélé involves several scrambles (Route 35)

From Refuge de l'Alpe descend south to the Plan de l'Alpe, in the valley of the Romanche, and walk upstream to where it forks at the Plan de Valfourche (2048m, 30mins). Curve left (south) on the route which continues to the Sources de la Romanche, as described at the end of Route 17. The way pushes on along the right-hand (west) side of the valley over moraines to a point at about 2312m where a cairn signals the start of the ascent to the Planchard hut.

Climbing steeply west in zigzags, the trail then slants right on a rising traverse to enter a shallow gully. Cairns and waymarks show the way up this, then out to scree and rock bands and a continuing path which mounts steeply again to a marker on a rocky crest. On gaining the marker post you should find the **Refuge Adèle Planchard** (3169m: *accommodation, refreshments*) nearby.

Take care on the descent, especially after rain, and allow 3hrs to return to the Alpe refuge.

Route 19: Refuge de l'Alpe (2079m) – Refuge du Pavé (2841m)

Grade:	3
Distance:	6½ kilometres (one way)
Height gain:	900 metres
Time:	3½hrs
Location:	WSW of Refuge de l'Alpe

Another walk between huts, this one has the bonus of a mountain tarn, Lac du Pavé, caught in a rock-rimmed basin near the refuge of the same name.

From the refuge take the path alongside the Romanche to where the valley forks at the Plan de Valfourche (described in Routes 17 and 18). Cross the footbridge by a signpost (2048m, 30mins) and follow the subsequent path that rises into the stony Cavales glen to the west. This attractive but wild little valley is headed by the pyramid-shaped Pic Nord des Cavales, with the Col du Clot des Cavales below that to the left. (This col is used by climbers moving between the Romanche and Étançons valleys.) Keeping on the right-hand side of the Torrent du Clot des Cavales, as the way progresses it steepens to mount the lateral moraine formed by the retreating Glacier du Clot. After a while descend to the right and continue upvalley to the end of the crest over old snow patches and fallen rocks. Maintain direction towards Pic Nord des Cavales, then rise in zigzags to a point below the Glacier du Clot where cairns direct a traverse northeast. With Lac du Pavé in view descend and cut round to the **Refuge du Pavé** (2841m: *accommodation, refreshments*). (Allow 2hrs for a return by the same path to Refuge de l'Alpe.)

Route 20: Refuge de l'Alpe (2079m) – Col d'Arsine (2340m)

Grade:	**1**
Distance:	**2½ kilometres (one way)**
Height gain:	**261 metres**
Time:	**1½hrs (45mins back)**
Location:	**Southeast of Refuge de l'Alpe**

Col d'Arsine is a long, broad saddle of grass and rocks, an easy walker's pass linking the valleys of the Romanche and Guisane used by the GR54 Tour de l'Oisans (see Route 22). It is also a popular destination in its own right at the head of a gently sloping pastoral valley, while the northeastern side drops sharply in a succession of natural steps to Le Casset on the Guisane.

A signpost at Refuge de l'Alpe gives 45mins to the col, but a more realistic time would be 1¼–1½hrs. The path is narrow but clear from the hut, rising above two simple Alp hutments, then through a grassy gully/trough alongside a small stream. Emerging to open pastures, Montagne des Agneaux and the Glacier d'Arsine are seen ahead beyond the col. At this point the GR54 trail is seen well to the left, while ours cuts ahead through pastures and crosses several minor streams on the way. It then veers left over stepping stones to join the main path. At the end of a long and gentle walk across near-level pastures, the trail climbs towards the pass, coming to the **Col d'Arsine** about 1¼hrs after leaving the refuge. Although the pass has plenty of attractive places on which to relax, an even better site will be found by descending on the far side for about 15mins to a truly delightful region where streams coming from the Glacier d'Arsine unite to form milky-blue oxbows – a footbridge gives access to the south side.

Route 21: Col d'Arsine (2340m) – Lac du Glacier d'Arsine (2455m)

Grade:	1
Distance:	1 kilometre (one way)
Height gain:	115 metres
Time:	30mins (45mins–1hr round trip)
Location:	Southeast of Refuge de l'Alpe

Seen to the right of Col d'Arsine a towering wall of moraine provides a somewhat desolate spectacle, but hidden behind it lies the milky glacial lake visited on this easy extension to Route 20.

At the col a signpost gives 45mins to the Lac du Glacier – a rather generous allowance! Bear right here and weave between rocks and boulders, making towards that moraine bank where a broad, well-made path angles across its face. The path slants left, gaining height without much effort, then swings to the right. Moments later it brings you to the glacial waters of the lake, backed by the dirty tongue of the Glacier d'Arsine. Above the glacier a long wall curves round from Pic de Neige Cordier (seen to the right) and Montagne des Agneaux. A variety of paths not shown on the map invite further exploration.

Route 22: Villar d'Arène (1683m) – Col d'Arsine (2340m) – Le Casset (1512m)

Grade:	2–3
Distance:	17 kilometres
Height gain:	657 metres
Height loss:	828 metres
Time:	5½–6hrs
Location:	Southeast of Villar d'Arène

VALLÉE DE LA ROMANCHE

*This classic crossing from the Romanche to the Guisane has already been
mentioned as being an integral part of the Tour de l'Oisans, but it could
also be used as a day-walk by non-backpackers, with a return arranged
either by car or bus from Le Casset or Monêtier-les-Bains.*

Begin by following Route 15 from Villar d'Arène to Refuge de
l'Alpe (2¼hrs), and from there to **Col d'Arsine**, as described in
Route 20 (total 3hrs 45mins). From the pass the well-marked path
descends northeast, losing about 100m to an attractive area where
drainage streams from the Glacier d'Arsine snake through lawn-
like levels. After this the trail passes below a shepherd's hut and
continues down with consistently fine views of the stream, which is
either crystal clear or milky-blue. Natural rock gardens line the way,
and having lost height without any severe gradients the path
suddenly descends steeply and, with a small lake in view, it forks.
The right-hand option takes a less-demanding course than the alternative, while the left-hand trail swoops down in tight zigzags. The
two reunite just before the path crosses a waterfall. A few minutes
later come to Lac de la Douche (1900m, 4hrs 50mins), a very
popular site with picnic parties.

Soon after leaving the lake and crossing a rocky area, the path
enters larchwoods and breaks into several braidings. A pleasant
woodland walk, with occasional open glades, the way leads to a
stream crossing (Le Petit Tabuc) and onto a track (1683m). Easy
walking takes you along the track, swinging downvalley in long
loops, then crossing to the left bank of the stream at 1569m, about
15mins after first joining it. A dirt road now leads directly into **Le
Casset** (1512m: *accommodation, refreshments*) a little over 2hrs from
Col d'Arsine.

Le Casset has an épicerie (foodstore), bar/café and gîte d'étape, Gîte du
Casset: 24 places, open end June to end Sept, and mid-Dec to end April
(☎ 04 92 24 45 74). There is an infrequent bus service to La Grave and Bourg
d'Oisans across Col du Lautaret, and to Briançon in the other direction.

VALLÉE DE LA GUISANE

Broad and sunny, with more than a brief nod to the ski industry, the lower half of the Vallée de la Guisane offers a range of summer activities beyond those of walking, trekking and climbing – canoeing, mountain biking and paragliding among them. Bold crags wall the upper reaches, and high trails seek out remote corners; in early summer swamps of flowers and sudden surprise views reward the walker.

ACCESS AND INFORMATION

Location: Southeast of Col du Lautaret, the valley of the Guisane drains down to the Durance, which it joins at Briançon, forming the northeast boundary of the Écrins region

Bases: Le Casset (1512m), Monêtier-les-Bains (1495m), Briançon (1253m)

Information: Parc National des Écrins Information Office, Le Casset

Office du Tourisme, Monêtier-les-Bains (☎ 04 92 24 41 98)

Office du Tourisme, La Salle-les-Alpes (☎ 04 92 24 71 88)

Office du Tourisme, St-Chaffrey (☎ 04 92 24 09 46)

Office du Tourisme, Maison des Templiers, Briançon (☎ 04 92 21 08 50)

Access: From the Vallée de la Romanche (Bourg d'Oisans/La Grave) over Col du Lautaret via N91, or from Briançon. Infrequent daily bus service operates between Bourg d'Oisans and Briançon. Briançon has mainline rail links with Paris.

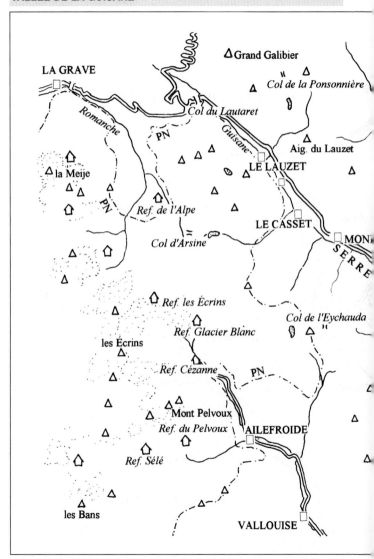

VALLÉE DE LA GUISANE

INTRODUCTION

This broad valley, which links the Romanche with the Haute-Durance, is peripheral to the main Écrins region, and its main purpose, as far as this guidebook is concerned, is one of access. That is not to suggest, however, that it holds no interest to the walker. On the contrary, it has a wide range of possibilities, a brief sample of day walks being given below. Long-distance routes such as GR50 (Tour du Haut-Dauphiné) and GR57 (Autour de Névache) sample some of the valley's delights, and GR5 overlooks the southeastern end. The Tour de l'Oisans (GR54) makes a tentative entry by descending from Col d'Arsine to Le Casset (Route 22), and leaves again via Monêtier-les-Bains and Col de Eychauda (Route 24), while in winter the Guisane comes into its own as a popular venue for cross-country skiing (*ski de fond*).

On the journey from Col du Lautaret the road skirts the southern slopes of the 3228m Grand Galibier, after which the valley opens and villages come into view ahead. Between the Lautaret and Briançon there are 13 villages and hamlets on either side of the road. Off to the right a reddish scar on the hillside betrays an exposed salt lick, where in the early mornings large herds of chamois can be found. Nearby a small hamlet, Le Lauzat, lies just below the road, as does the first village a short distance beyond it, Le Casset. But the remaining villages on the way to Briançon are all gathered around the N91 and grouped together under the generic heading of Serre-Chevalier: including Monêtier-les-Bains, Villeneuve, La Salle, Chantemerle and St-Chaffrey.

Serre-Chevalier claims to enjoy 300 days of sunshine a year, and is the largest and most northerly of winter resorts in the Southern Alps, with a variety of lifts and tows reaching 2500m. Most of the ski complex (the Grand Serre-Che) is concentrated on the southern slopes of the valley, pushing close to the national park boundary and leaving the northern hillsides mostly piste-free for the walker to enjoy.

On that northern hillside a minor road loops back and forth above Chantemerle to gain the walling ridge at Col de Granon (2404m). A short walk then leads to an observation point for a panoramic view across the valley to La Meije, Barre des Écrins, Mont Pelvoux (see Appendix B) and others. At the upper, north-western, end of this walling ridge lies the impressive rock-buttressed Massif du Cerces, a fine walking and climbing area encircled by GR57.

Forest covers the southern flank of the valley to a height of around 2000m, with barren mountains rising above the treeline. Few of the summits reach 3000m and only one remnant glacier (that of Prés les Fonts) lies outside the national park. With the aid of *téléphérique* to the Serre-Chevalier mountain, ridge-walks and circuits can be made which link up with ski pistes – easy walking, but in a badly-scarred landscape. One or two narrow minor roads snake through the lower forest, while paths cross cols that provide access to the inner glens and valleys of the Écrins massif.

MAIN VALLEY BASES

- **LE CASSET** (1512m) is only a small village at the upper end of the valley, but it's an important staging post on GR54, as well as having easy access to GR50 on the northern hillside. Le Casset spans the Guisane river, and its modest facilities include a grocery, bar/café and a *gîte d'étape*. There's also a national park information office, open in summer only. Note that there is no campsite here, despite the symbol indicating one on the IGN map, although 'wild' camping is permitted on specific and fairly obvious sites along the river bank between here and Monêtier.

- **MONÊTIER-LES-BAINS** (1495m) – also known as Serre-Chevalier 1500 – is a ski resort and spa, whose hot springs were known to the Romans. It has a *gîte* and several hotels, restaurants, shops, bank (infrequently open), PTT and tourist information office.

- **BRIANÇON** (1253m) is Europe's highest town, with a population of about 11,000. Situated at the confluence of four valleys (Guisane, Clarée, Durance and Cerveyrette), it is a happy mix of medieval and modern whose *ville haute* was walled by Vauban for Louis XIV following a fire which destroyed much of the town in 1692. Briançon has all modern services, including a hospital, many hotels and a *gîte d'étape*. The railway station is at the southern end of town. Just outside Briançon, marking the junction of the Guisane and Clarée valleys, the rock spur of Croix de Toulouse gives an excellent overview of Vauban's fortifications, as well as a very fine impression of the Vallée de la Guisane as far as the Col du Lautaret. Croix de Toulouse also has a 680m *via ferrata*, which mounts the cliff in about 4hrs to end a little east of the 1962m summit.

OTHER VALLEY BASES

Accommodation may be found in assorted villages along the valley, mostly in the Serre-Chevalier chain, although – being primarily aimed at the ski market – not everything is open in summer. In addition to those already mentioned, there's a *gîte d'étape* above **LE LAUZAT** (Halte de Roche Robert: open in summer: ☎ 04 92 20 20 90) and another just below the N91 at **LES BOUSSARDES** (15 places: ☎ 04 92 24 42 13), and a youth hostel (*auberge de jeunesse*) at **LE BEZ** (open all year: ☎ 04 92 24 74 54).

MOUNTAIN HUTS

There are no mountain huts immediately accessible from the Vallée de la Guisane.

Route 23: Le Lauzat (1668m) –
Grand Lac (2282m) – Le Lauzat

Grade:	**2**
Distance:	**9 kilometres**
Height gain/loss:	**648 metres**
Time:	**5–5½hrs**
Location:	**Northwest of Le Casset**

The hamlet of Le Lauzat is situated some 3km upvalley from Le Casset, by which it is linked by the old Lautaret road. The N91 passes above the hamlet, crossing below a narrow hanging valley guarded by the Roche Robert (2399m) at the so-called Pont de l'Alpe. Walkers with their own transport will find several parking areas near Pont de l'Alpe, which will slightly reduce the route to Le Grand Lac. Above Alpe du Lauzat it's quite a strenuous walk, with a 50m scramble up a rock chimney safeguarded by a fixed cable.

From Le Lauzat go up the slope to the N91 road at Pont de l'Alpe and follow signs for Le Grand Lac along a track twisting uphill (GR50). After about 15mins the track forks. Take the left-hand, more narrow option which slopes down to the Torrent du Rif, where a sign directs the way to the Grand Lac and Col de la Ponsonnière. Shortly after, cross a bridge and take the right branch when the trail forks. The way curves north with Roche Robert above to the left, and rises through the short Vallon du Plan Chevalier towards what appears to be a saddle at its head.

Coming to a rock tip the trail picks a way through and eventually brings you to the foot of a rock chimney just below the saddle. A fixed cable eases the ascent and you emerge to a view southwest to the glacier-draped Montagne des Agneaux, which mostly hides the Barre des Écrins. A short descent is now made on the northern side to the **Grand Lac** (2282m, 2½–3hrs).

Wander along the right-hand (eastern) shore, but nearing the far end bear right to cut up the slope and join a section of GR57. The way now goes down into a broad hanging valley flanked on the right by the limestone Arêtes de la Bruyère and on the left by the Tête de la Cassille. The valley is drained by the infant Torrent du Rif, which is crossed on rocks. Now follow the stream through narrows, keeping on its left bank, and the way eventually brings you to **Alpe du Lauzat** (1940m: *accommodation, refreshments*), where you rejoin the GR50. This takes you down to Pont de l'Alpe with Le Lauzat seen just below.

Other Walks from Le Lauzat

- An extension to Route 23 carries the walk beyond Le Grand Lac to another, much smaller tarn near the head of the valley at 2565m, and from there up to the 2613m **COL DE LA PONSONNIÈRE** (40–60mins from Le Grand Lac). The final 100m to the col are somewhat exposed and caution is advised.

- Col de la Ponsonnière is crossed by walkers on GR57, while the west ridge (the Crête de la Ponsonnière) carries a grade 3 route to the summit of the 3228m **GRAND GALIBIER**. Marking the boundary between Savoie and Hautes-Alpes, the summit is a noted viewpoint. (Allow 4½–5hrs from Pont de l'Alpe to the Grand Galibier.)

- A third possibility from Le Lauzat is a **CIRCUIT OF AIGUIL-LETTE DU LAUZAT**. Begin by following GR50 to Alpe du Lauzat, and continue upvalley as far as the junction with GR57, where you turn right and climb to Col du Chardonnet at 2638m. Leave GR57 here and bear right on the west side of the Crête du Chardonnet. On reaching the ridge linking the crête with the Aiguillette du Lauzat, head west a short distance to Col de l'Aiguillette (2534m), then flank round the east side of the mountain and zigzag down to the GR50, which at this point follows the old military route of the so-called Chemin du Roy. A continuing steep descent could be pursued to Les Boussardes in the Guisane, or (a better option) turn right and follow GR50 back to Alpe du Lauzat and Pont de l'Alpe. This is a grade 2, 5hr circuit. (The limestone cliffs of the Aiguillette have been equipped with a *via ferrata*.)

- To the west of Le Lauzat the crags of the Pics de Combeynot form a steep backing. In a high cirque at 2555m a glacial tarn, **LAC DU COMBEYNOT**, is reached by a waymarked trail via Les Boussardes, along which it's often possible to see herds of chamois. Allow 5hrs for a there-and-back walk. Most of this route lies well within the Parc National des Écrins.

Walks from Serre-Chevalier

- The string of villages that comprise Serre-Chevalier, as noted in the introduction to this section, give access to walks on both sides of the valley. Those on the south slopes are mostly wooded, but the north flank has some high trails which look across to the giant peaks of the main Écrins massif. Of particular note is the **GRAND AREA**, a 2869m high point on the ridge separating the valleys of the Guisane and Clarée, gained by a very pleasant grade 1 route. The start of this walk is the Buvette Sainte-Joseph at 2171m, reached by the minor road (D234) which twists up the hillside from Chantemerle to Col de Granon. The trail climbs above the *buvette* (snack bar) to gain a ridge northwest of Le Petit Area, then follows this crest to the main summit (2½hrs). A tremendous 360° panoramic view from here includes the distant Mont Blanc in one direction, Monte Viso in another, while the major peaks and glaciers of the Écrins range crowd the western view.

• Below and to the northwest of Le Grand Area, the 2427m **COL DE BUFFÈRE** is one of several crossing points that enable walkers to move from the Guisane to the Vallée de la Clarée. This particular col is used by GR57 (Autour de Névache), and a good day's exercise could be had by simply walking to the col and back. For this it is sensible to begin in Le Freyssinet, a small village on the north side of the N91 a short distance downvalley from Monêtier. GR50 comes through the village, and this waymarked trail is followed uphill to the Alp huts of Le Puy Freyssinet, passing an old anthracite mine on the way. Beyond the hut ruins the trail twists uphill for another 200m or so to join the traverse path of GR57. Bear right and ease round the hillside, rising to the Col de Buffère about 3½hrs after leaving Le Freyssinet. (Allow 2hrs for a return by the same path.)

• The two-section **SERRE-CHEVALIER** *téléphérique*, which rises from Chantemerle, gives access to some high trails and pistes, as well as providing views of the Écrins from the 2491m summit, where there's an orientation table. A short (45min) and easy walk from the cableway station leads across Col de Serre Chevalier to the **SOMMET DE L'EYCHAUDA** (2659m). The northwest ridge of this mountain, known as the Crête de Roche Gauthier, provides a grade 3 walk/scramble to Col d'Eychauda, while the same col can be reached by an easier path from Serre Chevalier by way of Col de la Pisse (avoiding the Sommet de l'Eychauda). The trail from here gives very fine views into the deep Vallon de Chambran as it makes an airy traverse round to **COL DE L'EYCHAUDA** (2425m). One could then either continue west for 1¼hrs to gain the Rocher de l'Yret (2830m) overlooking Lac de l'Eychauda, complete a circular route by scrambling along the Crête de Roche Gauthier back to the *téléphérique* (1¾hrs from the col), or follow GR54 waymarks down to Monêtier-les-Bains for a 4–5hr walk.

Route 24: Le Casset (1512m) – Col de l'Eychauda (2425m) – Ailefroide (1507m)

Grade:	3
Distance:	21 kilometres
Height gain:	913 metres
Height loss:	918 metres
Time:	8hrs
Location:	South of Le Casset, over the mountains to the Vallée de la Vallouise

The majority of this long and demanding route is used by walkers tackling the Tour de l'Oisans, and it leads to one of the main mountaineering centres of the region. Ailefroide is almost perfectly placed for the exploration of some of the most dramatic country within the national park, and the walk to it trades the verdant Guisane landscape for a much more rugged terrain. In between it climbs through steep forest and out to a scarred and seemingly barren series of hillsides largely sacrificed to downhill skiing. In short, it's a walk of great variety and extremes.

From the church in Le Casset cross a bridge over the river and bear left on a path which cuts through meadows. After about 20mins come to a bridge over the Guisane, cross and turn right on a riverside footpath which leads to the outskirts of **Monêtier-les-Bains** (1495m, 30mins: *accommodation, refreshments*). Cross the Guisane again to its right bank, then turn left along a road. Shortly after passing a footbridge turn right on a narrow road between meadows, and when this reaches a parking area bear left on a track – a sign gives 3hrs to Col de l'Eychauda.

A short distance up this track take a footpath among trees on the right. It's quite a steep pull and it brings you to Charvet (1608m), a part-ruined house and a small chapel (Saint-Antoine) with a fine view of mountains on the north side of the valley. The path cuts alongside the buildings and into larchwoods, where it soon makes a long contour to the right and forks. Take the upper branch which now curves and forks again. Once more take the upper option, which is now the right branch. At the next fork take the right branch again – the lower of two paths. It contours a little, then cuts up alongside the Torrent de la Selle: a steep climb which eventually breaks to the right across an open glade to cross the stream (1980m, 2hrs).

Now climbing into a tight little valley you recross to the left side of the stream and eventually come to an ugly complex of ski tows, chairlifts and broad bulldozed pistes. The path has been disrupted, but its course goes up the left-hand side of a wide piste straight ahead. However, it is preferable to curve left at this point and go up to a saddle, where you turn right along a track, passing a ski building on the left. This track goes all the way to Col de l'Eychauda, with the GR54 path cutting across or running parallel with it. When the track forks do not take the right branch which swings round towards Pas de l'Ane, but go up more or less beneath the line of a chairlift. So come to the broad and grassy **Col de l'Eychauda** (2425m, 3½hrs).

Cross the col on a continuing track, but soon leave it in favour of a path which makes a long contour of the left flank of the Neyzets glen, before descending in numerous zigzags to the Vallon de Chambran. It's a steep descent, although the zigzags are generous, and it brings you onto a track in the bed of the valley about 1½hrs from the col. Turn left and wander down the track to the tiny hamlet of **Chambran** (1719m, 5¼–5½hrs: *refreshments*), where there's a *buvette* offering welcome refreshment.

The track is metalled from Chambran, and you continue along it for about 15mins until it curves a little to the left. Just beyond this a sign on the right indicates the start of a footpath descent to Pelvoux. (During research a section of this formerly splendid path had been overrun by a bulldozed track.) When the path (or track) forks, take the right-hand option which goes through trees and across a short sloping meadow and onto a track. Turn right, soon to cross the Chambran stream. When the track forks continue ahead, and after a while ignore a cairn on the left marking the point where a path breaks away to Pelvoux. Remain on the track, which contours pleasantly and soon presents a hint of big mountains and glaciers ahead.

The track ends where a large pipe enters the hillside as part of a hydro-electric scheme. A footpath now continues. Ignore an alternative path which zigzags up a rock slope, and continue ahead, rising to cross a grass and boulder bluff, then twisting a little higher beyond it, with views into the narrow wooded valley below. Having reached a high point at a rocky corner, the path slants downhill, gently at first, then more steeply with zigzags to pass below a prominent black crag. Beyond this come to an *abri*, or small stone shelter, beside a path junction. Take the left branch ahead, still sloping downhill. It then descends steeply to a prominent crossing path.

Turn right on what becomes a delightful contour. The path becomes a track by a chalet, and when it forks with a small meadow ahead, take the right branch (sign to Ailefroide par Pra Chapel). The track narrows to a footpath, and rising gently brings you to a broad but shallow stream tumbling down the mountainside. Pick your way across on rocks (there is no bridge) and continue between trees, the trail fringed with wild raspberries, and eventually arrive in **Ailefroide** (1507m, 7½–8hrs: *accommodation, refreshments*) on the north side of the bridge spanning the Torrent de St-Pierre. Turn left into the village.

Ailefroide has a huge campsite covering several locations. There are a few hotels, a gîte, shops and restaurants, PTT and a Bureau des Guides. An infrequent bus service links Ailefroide with Vallouise. See Vallée de la Vallouise section for further details and a range of walks in the neighbourhood.

VALLÉE DE LA VALLOUISE

The verdant landscapes of the lower valley contrast with savage rock walls that soar above Ailefroide and the open, glacier-scoured region of Pré de Madame Carle that lies below two major icefields. Valloise town enjoys light, space and distant views, but the valley between St-Antoine and Ailefroide is hemmed in between rough-hewn cliffs and dark forest. Tributaries to east and west add to the list of possibilities for walkers – an impressive list at that – while the arc of the high mountains that encloses the Vallée de la Vallouise is both complex and awesome.

ACCESS AND INFORMATION

Location: Southwest of the Guisane, the valley penetrates deep into the Écrins Massif. Its major river drains the Glacier Blanc, which curves round the Barre des Écrins and, as the Gyronde, flows roughly southeast to join the Durance at L'Argentière-la-Bessée

Bases: Vallouise (1166m), Ailefroide (1507m)

Information: Office du Tourisme de la Vallouise, Place de l'Église, 05290 Vallouise (☎ 04 92 23 36 12)

Maison du Parc, 05290 Vallouise (☎ 04 92 23 32 31)

Office du Tourisme, Les Alberts, 05290 Puy-St-Vincent (☎ 04 92 23 35 80)

Tourisme Informations du Pays des Écrins, 05120 L'Argentière-la-Bessée (☎ 04 92 23 03 11)

Access: Road access (D994E) from L'Argentière, 17km southwest of Briançon. L'Argentière has rail and bus links with Briançon. There's an infrequent bus service through the valley from Briançon to Vallouise, and on to Ailefroide and Pré de Madame Carle.

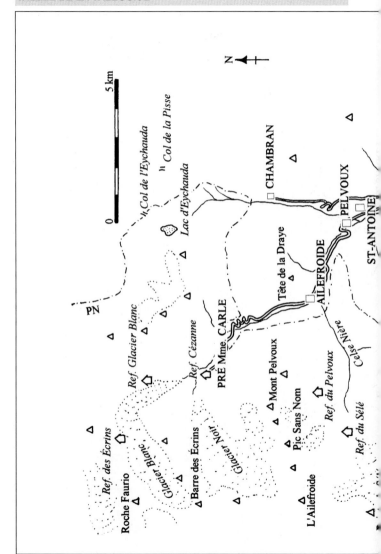

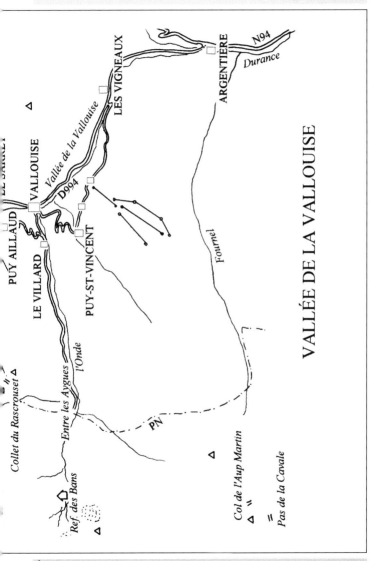

VALLÉE DE LA VALLOUISE

INTRODUCTION

Named in the 15th century after Louis XI, the Vallée de la Vallouise is an important tributary of the Durance, and has been recognised for 100 years or more as one of the region's major centres of mountaineering. With three feeder glens (those of the Onde, Chambran and Sélé – or Celse Nière) and the winter resort of Puy-St-Vincent on the slopes above Vallouise, it also attracts walkers, skiers and general tourists.

Entering the valley from L'Argentière, Mont Pelvoux (see Appendix B) comes briefly into view at La Bâtie. Les Vigneaux is the first real village, built on a curve in the valley below the Tête d'Aval. A 240m *via ferrata*, the Falaise de la Balme (fee payable), has been created on the outskirts of the village where a side road breaks away to climb through Les Prés and Les Alberts to Puy-St-Vincent. With the valley spread out below, Puy-St-Vincent has a splendid view of Mont Pelvoux, Glacier Blanc and Les Bans, among others, and although noted primarily as a ski resort equipped with a variety of mechanical lifts and 30km of cross-country pistes, it's of interest in summer too, with walking trails and a 200m *via ferrata* on the Plateau de Tournoux.

Back in the valley bed the D994E rises alongside the river and comes to Vallouise in a sunny, triangular plain at the confluence of the Onde and the Gyronde. A secondary road, D804, twists up the southern hillside to Puy-St-Vincent, while another (D504) projects westward into the valley of the Onde (Vallée d'Entraigue). A small but attractive market town, Vallouise is the main centre for the valley, although it's a little too far from the visually dramatic country that makes the region so special to be the first choice as a base for experienced mountain walkers.

Straying west from Vallouise, the valley of the Onde is narrow and heavily wooded at first, but at the hamlet of Le Villard (the only one in this glen) it momentarily opens with a teasing view towards its head. An unmanned campsite, with basic facilities only, is located on the south bank at Pont des Places (3km from Vallouise), and the road ends at Entre les Aygues, about 5km further on. This roadhead is the start of two major trails: one which pushes straight ahead to Refuge des Bans; the other being the route of GR54, which heads south on a fairly long crossing of the mountains to Refuge du

Pré de la Chaumette. A third, but less-frequented, option climbs north from Entre les Aygues on a steep climb that tackles the Collet du Rascrouset (2799m) as an energetic way of reaching the Vallon de la Sélé and Ailefroide.

The standard route to Ailefroide from Vallouise, however, continues along D994E, which leaves the town heading north to a string of small villages, most of which offer accommodation of one sort or another to summer visitors, while the left-hand hillside has a second ski area on the slopes of La Blanche above Puy Allaud.

At Le Sarret D421T snakes up the right-hand (eastern) hillside in a series of hairpin bends with views of Mont Pelvoux and its neighbours, Pic Sans Nom and L'Ailefroide. Almost 500m above the Gyronde this minor road enters the Vallon de Chambran, a high glacier-carved valley from which two or three energetic walking possibilities are worth considering.

Meanwhile, the main valley road passes through St-Antoine and Les Claux, both now collectively renamed Pelvoux. This small village stands astride D994E with Mont Pelvoux towering above it to the northwest – an impressive sight. Immediately beyond the village mountain walls crowd in on the valley. Its lower slopes are wooded, the river, known here as the Torrent d'Ailefroide, rushing among rocks and boulders as the road grinds up past the initial camping grounds of Ailefroide village which, after La Bérarde, is *the* main climbing base in the Écrins Massif. The great rock slabs that soar out of the valley just outside the village have long been noted as a climber's playground, and are now adorned with numerous bolted sport routes.

At Ailefroide the left-hand walls of the valley are pushed back a little by the Vallon de la Sélé, which breaks away to the southwest, thus giving the village the light and sense of space it needs. A short side road provides access to a large open camping meadow at the entrance to this glen, beyond which a good path progresses into the national park and, out of forest, advances to the valley's wild upper reaches; another trail crosses the river and climbs into the hanging Vallon de Clapouse for a full-frontal view of Mont Pelvoux's South Face.

Out of Ailefroide the upper valley road, now numbered D204T, rises in hairpins to an open, sunny but stony plain with a huge car park at Pré de Madame Carle (1874m), named after the widow of Godefroy Carle, President of Dauphiné under Louis XII. It's an awesome site, and one that attracts hordes of visitors on every bright day in summer. Waterfalls cascade into the larch- and birch-clad basin; glacial slabs directly ahead appear to support the snout of Glacier Blanc, while to the left the great lateral moraine of the Glacier Noir largely disguises the rubble-strewn icefield which fills the valley between Mont Pelvoux and the Barre des Écrins (see Appendix B). For many the space around Refuge Cézanne at the northern edge of the car park is the limit of ambition, but for walkers a close view of the glaciers is irresistable. There are, of course, trails to satisfy most needs throughout the valley.

MAIN VALLEY BASES

- **VALLOUISE** (1166m) is a busy but attractive little town with some pleasant buildings and a weekly produce market held on Thursdays. It has four hotels, two *gîtes d'étape*, a large campsite, tourist office, PTT (foreign exchange available), and several shops, restaurants and bars. There's also a Maison du Parc National des Écrins open throughout the year. Minibus services run to Ailefroide, Pré de Madame Carle, Entre les Aygues, Chambran and L'Argentière-la-Bessée. The Office du Tourisme publishes a *Petit guide pratique* giving details of accommodation, etc, throughout the valley – write or phone for a copy.

- **AILEFROIDE** (1507m) is much smaller than Vallouise, but with a true mountain atmosphere. The extensive camping grounds (open mid-June to mid-Sept) stretch north, south and west of the village – the reception office is at the southern, wooded end. The one-street village has two hotels (Chalet Hôtel Rolland and Hôtel Engilberge – both two star) and a *gîte d'étape*, several restaurants/snack bars, two groceries, climbing equipment shops and a Bureau des Guides (☎ 04 92 23 32 02).

OTHER VALLEY BASES

As mentioned above, practically every village in the Vallée de la Vallouise offers some form of accommodation. The following list is not comprehensive, but gives an idea of what's available. **LES VIGNEAUX** has a *gîte d'étape* with 40 places (Le Mont Brison ☎ 04 92 23 10 99) and no less than three campsites. **LE GRAND PARCHER**, between Les Vigneaux and Vallouise, also has a *gîte d'étape* on a 17th-century farm: La Tête d'Aval (24 places, ☎ 04 92 23 55 55).

Above Vallouise **PUY AILLAUD** has a 40-place *gîte d'étape* (☎ 04 92 23 37 32), open all year, while at **PELVOUX** (**ST-ANTOINE** and **LES CLAUX**) there's a choice of five hotels, a large campsite (Le Freyssinet) open from mid-June to mid-September, and a swimming pool.

MOUNTAIN HUTS

Some of the most exhilerating walks in and around the Vallée de la Vallouise are those that visit mountain refuges, most of which are set in magnificent surroundings. Please note that in summer it is *essential* to book in advance if accommodation is required – although not if you plan to visit just for refreshment.

- **REFUGE DU PRÉ DE LA CHAUMETTE** (1790m) is actually located well outside the Vallouise region near the head of the pastoral Vallée du Drac de Champoléon, but is included here as it is reached in a reasonably long day's effort from Entre les Aygues by walkers tackling GR54, and that section of the walk is described below. This comfortable, well-equipped refuge is owned by the Gap section of the CAF, can sleep 60 in its dormitories and has a guardian in summer (☎ 04 92 55 95 34).

- **REFUGE DES BANS** (2076m) is nicely situated less than 2hrs walk from Entre les Aygues, the roadhead in the Vallée de l'Onde (otherwise known as the Vallée d'Entraigue). It is owned by the Briançon section of the CAF, and has 22 places and a guardian in summer (☎ 04 92 23 39 48). Les Bans rises above the hut to the northwest, while a view south across the valley shows Pic de Bonvoisin and its hanging glaciers.

- **REFUGE DU SÉLÉ** (2511m) is architecturally hideous, a modernistic bunker – but a comfortable one, also owned by the

Briançon section of the CAF. It stands on a rock barrier near the head of the Vallon de la Sélé southwest of Ailefroide, from which it's gained in about 3–3½hrs – the final approach is by way of a fixed-rope-aided scramble up rock slabs. With a guardian in summer, the refuge has 76 spaces and a full meals service (☎ 04 92 23 39 49).

- **REFUGE DU PELVOUX** (2704m) is a well-appointed hut located on a rock shelf high above the Vallon de la Sélé, about 3½–4hrs from Ailefroide. Yet again, this is owned by the Briançon section of the CAF, has 58 places and is wardened in summer (☎ 04 92 23 39 47).

- **CHALET-HOTEL REFUGE CÉZANNE** (1874m) – also known as the Chalet-Refuge du Pré de Madame Carle – is privately owned and stands on the edge of the roadhead car park at Pré de Madame Carle. It is open in summer, and provides 40 places and a restaurant service (☎ 04 92 23 44 21).

- **REFUGE DU GLACIER BLANC** (2543m) is a large stone building perched on a crown of rock adjacent to the Glacier Blanc icefall. One of the most heavily used huts in the Écrins, and visited by crowds of walkers in summer, the setting is very fine indeed – about 2hrs from Pré de Madame Carle. CAF-owned (Briançon section) and with 135 spaces, the refuge is wardened winter and summer (☎ 04 92 23 50 24).

- **REFUGE DES ÉCRINS** (3170m) is located another 2½hrs beyond the Glacier Blanc refuge – ice axe recommended – standing on rocks overlooking the glacier and with the Barre des Écrins in view to the southwest. This is another exceptionally busy CAF hut, almost exclusively for climbers, with 105 places (often sleeping as many as 200); it is manned in summer and has a full meals service (☎ 04 92 23 46 66).

Route 25: Entre les Aygues (1604m) – Col de l'Aup Martin (2761m) – Pas de la Cavale (2735m) – Refuge de la Chaumette (1790m)

Grade:	3
Distance:	13 kilometres
Height gain:	1205 metres
Height loss:	1030 metres
Time:	7–7½hrs
Location:	Southwest of Vallouise

This long and fairly demanding route is another of those crossings adopted by GR54 (the Tour de l'Oisans), and Col de l'Aup Martin is the highest pass on that circuit. According to a footnote in A.W. Moore's **The Alps in 1864,** *this route is a 'military road [which] leads over the Pas de la Cavale to Champoléon'. Assuming you've been using Vallouise as a base, the first thing to consider is how to get to Entre les Aygues to begin the walk – unless, that is, you have a vehicle and plan to return by the same route in a day or so, in which case you can leave it at the roadhead. From Vallouise you could try hitching, taxi or use the minibus service (check at the tourist office for timetables). The other option, of course, is to walk all the way – allow 2½–3hrs for this.*

At the roadhead of Entre les Aygues (refreshments at the *buvette*) descend to the river and cross by footbridge. A trail winds among trees and bushes, and improves as you enter the narrow Vallon de la Selle heading south then southwest. Keeping the stream on your left the way makes height easily at first, and after an hour or so passes the Cabane (or Refuge) du Jas Lacroix (1946m). Beyond the refuge the path bears left and crosses a tributary stream draining the Chanteloube cirque, whose upper ridge is adorned with glacial remnants.

Now the way climbs into a high pastureland basin rimmed by a skyline of rocky peaklets wearing aprons of scree, and the path runs along its right-hand side, crossing several side streams before becoming more stony as height is gained towards the next 'step' in the valley. Once this is gained the col can be seen, with the continuing path slanting across long fans of black scree that demand caution. Across this scree you come onto the **Col de l'Aup**

Refuge du Pré de la Chaumette (Route 25) is used by walkers on the Tour of the Osians

Martin (2761m), about 2½–3hrs from the roadhead. Views are very fine, despite the proximity of any major peaks. Across the secretive little valley on the far side the mountain face is patterned with a contorted strata, while the next pass to cross, Pas de la Cavale, lies off to the right across yet more slopes of scree and rock.

It should only take about 15mins to reach **Pas de la Cavale** (2735m), but the way to it involves negotiating a ledge directly beneath a small cascade – a shower is inevitable. Over the pass the trail is broad and easy to begin with, but as you lose height so the gradient steepens and, in places, is narrow and exposed, especially across a rock band, but beyond this the way zigzags remorselessly down towards the green and pastoral glen in which the hut is set. However, from a first sighting it will take more than an hour to reach it. Eventually the trail eases onto fairly level ground, there's a stream to cross, and just over this you enter the **Refuge du Pré de la Chaumette** (1790m: *accommodation, refreshments*).

Note: For the continuing route across the mountains to the Valgaudemar, as per GR54, please see Routes 39 and 40. However, the shortest and easiest way out of the mountains from Ref. Chaumette is to descend through the valley to Pont du Fossé, where the D944 leads to the main Gap–Grenoble road.

Route 26: Entre les Aygues (1604m) – Refuge des Bans (2076m)

Grade:	2
Distance:	4 kilometres (one way)
Height gain:	472 metres
Time:	1hr 45mins (3hrs round trip)
Location:	WSW of Vallouise

This is an undemanding walk, but both the valley it journeys through and the views from the hut make it a justifiably popular one.

A signpost at the western end of the Entre les Aygues parking area in the Vallée de l'Onde (Vallée d'Entraigue) marks the start of the path, suggesting 2hrs for the walk to the hut. There is a *buvette* nearby, offering refreshments in summer. At first the trail goes among larch and silver birch trees on the north side of a gravelly plain, with no discernible gain in height, but after 10mins the way begins to rise in long switchbacks. The trees gradually thin out, with the head of the valley showing as a ragged ridge spreading from Les Bans over Pic des Aupillous to Pic Jocelme and Pic de Bonvoisin, their upper flanks draped with minor glaciers or snow patches. It is this ridge which forms the divide between the Vallée de la Vallouise and that of Valgaudemar.

Topping a rise the hut may be detected some way ahead, seen end-on, perched on a rocky knoll, its white-painted shutters appearing like daubs of snow. Midway along the valley you cross a small pasture with streams flowing from the right; large boulders litter the upper pastureland slopes. Then you come to a pool beside the trail, a place noted for tadpoles and frogs, beyond which there are more streams to negotiate and rock clutters. The trail angles below the hut on its south side, and is aided by fixed cables where it cuts along easy ledges. Then you cut back to the right for a few paces to gain the **Refuge des Bans** (2076m: *accommodation, refreshments*).

This small refuge has a guardian in summer, when a simple meals service is offered. Towards the end of the season or in bad weather, if there are no bookings, it may be unmanned.

Route 27: Entre les Aygues (1604m) – Collette du Rascrouset (2799m) – Ailefroide (1507m)

Grade:	3
Distance:	10 kilometres
Height gain:	1195 metres
Height loss:	1292 metres
Time:	6½–7hrs
Location:	West and northwest of Vallouise

The north wall of the Vallée de l'Onde, or d'Entraigue, is steep and uncompromising when viewed from the valley. But above Entre les Aygues it has been grooved by the shallow Vallon du Riou du Gerpa, the head of which crests the ridge at Collette du Rascrouset. The north side of this ridge falls among snow patches, boulder tips and screes into the Vallon de Clapouse, which in turn eases to a larch-topped bluff with a grandstand view of Mont Pelvoux and mountain walls that erupt from the Vallée de la Vallouise above Ailefroide. The crossing of this ridge is a fairly serious undertaking and should only be attempted by experienced mountain walkers in good settled conditions.

From the parking area of Entre les Aygues the path to Refuge des Bans pushes ahead and is signposted. The path to Collette du Rascrouset breaks off to the right among trees and rocks, and soon crosses the Riou du Gerpa stream to its west side. Rising a little the way then cuts back to recross the stream and zigzags steeply uphill. As you gain height you can see back through the Vallon de la Selle to the south. Following cairns you once more cross the stream and soon resume climbing, now on the west slope.

About 500m above Entre les Aygues the way starts to move towards the centre of the corrie, still climbing over increasingly rough ground, and enters the national park (red, white and blue markers). The way continues, guided by cairns towards the foot of a rock barrier, and crosses the stream for the last time. Now begins a long rising traverse to the right of the rock barrier, which at last comes onto the **Collette du Rascrouset** (2799m, 4hrs) midway between Pointe du Rascrouset (on the left) and Point de Clapouse on the right. Directly ahead you have an overview of the wild and rocky little Vallon de Clapouse.

The initial descent demands a cautious approach over old snowfields that spill into a barren region of rocks and scree. There's no path as such, but cairns direct the way, keeping mostly left of centre of the rocky scoop, and as you lose height so the way improves. There are some short but steep descents, and on these you should pick your way with care. But at last you arrive at a more welcoming site where there's grass and a stream, and the corrie opens to give an unrestricted view of Mont Pelvoux ahead.

Follow the path which rises a little above the stream, skirts round the larch-crowned bluff of the Bosse de Clapouse, and resumes the descent, now among trees and shrubs and flowers. In direct contrast to the earlier descent, this is a lovely green and fragrant hillside, with a good path leading all the way down into the Vallon de la Sélé. Cross a footbridge over the river at 1572m and turn right on a crossing path. This takes you through woodland, then onto a minor road by the side of a campsite. Follow the road downvalley to **Ailefroide** (1507m: *accommodation, refreshments*).

Route 28: Chambran (1719m) – Lac d'Eychauda (2514m)

Grade:	2
Distance:	5 kilometres (one way)
Height gain:	795 metres
Time:	2½–3hrs (4½hrs round trip)
Location:	North of Vallouise

VALLÉE DE LA VALLOUISE

Trapped in a wild and remote hollow rimmed by the Crête des Grangettes, Dôme de Monêtier and Pic Gardiner, among others, Lac d'Eychauda is a popular destination for walkers based in the Vallée de la Vallouise. The route to it is moderately steep, but nowhere difficult.

Begin at the Chalets de Chambran, reached by the narrow D421T road which climbs out of the valley at Le Sarret, almost 2km upstream from Vallouise. For walkers without transport there's a minibus service from Vallouise during the high summer period – check at the tourist office for details.

From **Chambran** (*refreshments*) walk along the track which extends through the glen beyond the chalets – the Vallon de Chambran is an almost level pastoral valley banked by steep mountain walls – a popular suntrap. After about 15mins the way forks near some ruins. A sign here gives 2hrs 45mins to the lake; 2½hrs to Col de l'Eychauda. Ignore the path which cuts off to the right (GR54 – Route 29), but follow round to the very head of the glen where the track rises in easy twists. Entering the national park cross a bridge and then leave the track for a path on the right, which short-cuts a few bends. The trail zigzags to gain height, mounts a rock slab (cairns) and soon after brings you to the lake.

In the early summer there may be ice floating in the water. Under a dull sky the scene can be a little bleak, with sombre screes and rock walls as a backing. But if you go round the right-hand (east) shore the setting improves, with the Glacier de Séguret Foran seen hanging across the water.

Descend to Chambran by the same path used on the ascent (1¾–2hrs).

Note: Some 370m above the lake Col des Grangettes (2684m) is a tempting viewpoint for strong mountain walkers to aim for. A path rises steeply from the northeast shore and makes directly for the col in about 30mins. The view is very fine, not only across the cirque to the glacier peaks, but over the Vallée de la Guisane to Mont Thabor and a sea of peaks in the north and east. On the north side of the col a continuing path descends to Monêtier-les-Bains in the Vallée de la Guisane in about 3hrs.

Route 29: Chambran (1719m) –
Col de l'Eychauda (2425m)

Grade:	2
Distance:	6 kilometres (one way)
Height gain:	706 metres
Time:	2½hrs (4hrs round trip)
Location:	North of Vallouise

Col de l'Eychauda is traversed by walkers on the Tour de l'Oisans, on the stage from Le Casset or Monêtier to Ailefroide or Vallouise, and is described in Route 24 as a north–south crossing. Walkers based in the Vallée de la Vallouise, however, would not normally tackle that route, so the following description is included as a day-walk beginning at the Chalets de Chambran. To reach these, see directions in Route 28 above.

From the **Chambran** buildings (*refreshments*) walk upvalley along the track which projects north from the end of the metalled road, and after about 15mins branch right on a waymarked path signed to Col de l'Eychauda in 2½hrs. The path (GR54) climbs the steep grassy hillside in long switchbacks to enter a hidden upper glen, the Ravin des Neyzets. This is another pastoral hanging valley, with the col at the far end. Zigzags take the path up the right flank, then the way contours roughly northward, being joined by another trail from Col de la Pisse. Just before reaching the col the path comes onto a track which crosses at the col itself.

The upper slopes of many of the surrounding mountains have been scarred by the ski industry, but the bulldozed pistes and jeep tracks could be adopted for continuing tours in the vicinity of **Col de l'Eychauda**. To the southeast of the col, the 2491m Serre Chevalier has a *téléphérique* link with Chantemerle in the Guisane valley.

Route 30: Vallouise (1166m) – Torrent de Gyronde – Vallouise

Grade:	1
Distance:	4 kilometres
Height gain/loss:	68 metres
Time:	1–1¼hrs
Location:	North of Vallouise

A pleasant, easy riverside circuit for a summer's evening, this walk follows the Gyronde to a bridge below Le Sarret on the east bank and returns by an undulating path on the opposite side of the river.

From the bridge in the centre of Vallouise walk along the track which takes you upstream on the right-hand side of the **Gyronde**. It's an easy, gentle track, and as the river is popular with white-water canoeists, there's a chance that you might see some kayaks come racing downstream. At other times keep alert for sight of dippers plunging into the water. After a while the track narrows and takes you through a patch of trees, and 25–30mins from the start you come to a bridge and cross to the west bank. Over the bridge ignore the track heading to the right, and instead bear left to a path signed to Vallouise and Puy Aillaud, a hamlet several hundred metres up the hillside.

Soon after the path forks, with one breaking to the right for Puy Aillaud. For Vallouise, however, remain on the lower path, which traces an undulating course above the river, sometimes among trees, often in the open with tufts of lavender growing on the hillside. Nearing Vallouise the path suddenly climbs and forks once more. Again take the lower option onto a track which slopes down to a road. Bear left and follow this into **Vallouise**, which you enter near the 15th-century village church.

West of Refuge Sélé, the valley is a scene of barren splendour (Route 36)

The mountain wall (Pelvoux to L'Ailefroide) and Glacier Noir (Route 37)

Refuge du Glacier Blanc (Route 38)

Trekkers tackling the eroded ribs below Col de Vallonpierre (Route 39)

South to Vallonpierre from the head of the Valgaudemar (Routes 40, 41)

Domestic goats, seen near Le Bourg (Route 40)

The Valgaudemar between Villar-Loubière and La Chapelle (Route 48)

The hamlet of Pelvoux (formerly Les Claux) squats below the mountain from which it takes its name (Route 31)

Route 31: Vallouise (1166m) – St-Antoine (1250m) – Ailefroide (1507m)

Grade:	1–2
Distance:	7½ kilometres
Height gain:	341 metres
Time:	2¼–2½hrs
Location:	North of Vallouise

This walk to Ailefroide manages to avoid the main road for all but a very short stretch, and gives a surprisingly entertaining half-day's outing. The first stage, as far as St-Antoine, follows the river, but from Pelvoux it takes a higher path and mule-track partially through woodland.

Follow directions as for Route 30 along the east bank of the river for about 25–30mins. On coming to the bridge below Le Sarret cross to the west bank and turn right along the continuing track. This makes for easy walking, and it soon brings you to some buildings shown on the IGN map as a *village de vacances*. Here you join a service road and pass a swimming pool to your left. Just beyond this, one road branches right to the main village of St-Antoine, but we continue ahead towards the municipal campsite. Walk through the campsite, then bear right to cross a bridge and come to the upper part of **St-Antoine** (1250m, 1hr: *accommodation, refreshments*) near Hotel le Belvedere.

Turn left along the road and before long walk through **Pelvoux** (Les Claux, 1300m: *accommodation, refreshments*). On the outer edge of the village take a path on the right signed 'Ailefroide par Pra Chapel'. This forks in a few paces. Continue over a large water pipe, now on an old paved mule-path which rises steadily until easing to contour past a solitary chalet. Here the path becomes a track, and when this forks, you take the right-hand option and shortly after pass the Pra Chapel chalet.

The track narrows and becomes a footpath; rising a little it comes to a stream which is crossed on rocks. Continue along the path among trees and, passing below rock slabs, this will bring you onto the road on the north side of **Ailefroide** (1507m: *accommodation, refreshments*). Turn left to enter the main village.

Route 32: Ailefroide (1507m) – Tête de la Draye (2077m)

Grade:	3
Distance:	3 kilometres (one way)
Height gain:	570 metres
Time:	1¾–2hrs (3hrs round trip)
Location:	Northeast of Ailefroide

The vegetated promontory of the Tête de la Draye is a noted viewpoint, situated directly above Ailefroide at the base of a long and rocky ridge, and reached by a steep path providing bird's-eye views onto the village. Opposite, to the southwest, lies the Vallon de la Sélé (or Celse Nière), while upvalley to the northwest Glacier Blanc can be seen draining towards Pré de Madame Carle.

The walk begins about 20m upstream of the Pont Jean Vidal, the bridge spanning the river (the St Pierre) on the north side of Ailefroide. Branching right as a track, it is signed to Tête de la Draye (2hrs) and Les Claux (40mins). Passing between buildings a path then veers right and leads to the popular practice crags. At the second fork, by a rock slab, take the upper, left-hand path option, and when it forks again a few paces later, once more take the left branch (sign). The path now climbs steeply with tight zigzags, at first among trees, before making a long left slant up the hillside, with views directly down onto the rooftops of Ailefroide and upvalley, where the Glacier Blanc is the most prominent feature.

When the trail makes a brief descent and forks, take the upper right-hand option. This is a little scrambly for a brief spell, but it soon eases again and continues as an airy rake across the steep hillside. At an altitude of about 1870m you come to the Pissette stream and climb directly alongside it to gain another 30m, where the path forks yet again. Do not cross the stream, but continue up for a few more steps, then the way angles off to the right, makes a few zigzags among trees and alpenroses, but also contours here and there with fine views into the Vallon de la Sélé. Without any further effort of note the path brings you onto the grassy shoulder/ promontory of the **Tête de la Draye**.

The panorama displayed rewards the effort required to get there. Not only are the Vallon de la Sélé and associated Vallon de Clapouse open to view but also the busy-looking Vallée de la Vallouise, stretching to the southeast with distant peaks of the Queyras as a backdrop. The big block of Mont Pelvoux looms at the junction of the Sélé and Ailefroide valleys, and the Glacier Blanc gleams from the northwest.

Descend to Ailefroide by the same path, taking care to avoid knocking stones onto climbers below.

Route 33: Ailefroide (1507m) – Bosse de Clapouse (2179m)

Grade:	2
Distance:	4 kilometres (one way)

Height gain:	672 metres
Time:	2hrs (3½hrs round trip)
Location:	Southwest of Ailefroide

Seen from close quarters the Vallon de Clapouse is a wild, scree-cluttered hanging valley (see Route 27) which drains into the Celse Nière, or Vallon de la Sélé, southwest of Ailefroide. From Ailefroide itself the glen looks very enticing, its entrance guarded by a larch-topped bluff, its walling ridges topped by ragged summits above long scree fans. From the Sélé valley one of the attractions is a waterfall which sprays down its southern wall from the Vallon de Clapouse, and this cascade starts virtually at the Bosse de Clapouse. The walk up through sparse larch-woods to the Bosse is an engaging one which provides a number of good viewpoints, but the best of all will be found on arrival.

At the upper end of Ailefroide's single street a minor road breaks off to the southwest by the entrance to Hotel Engilberge and immediately enters the Vallon de la Sélé, which at this point is open with large meadows interspersed with larch trees. The road goes as far as a camping ground and ends at a parking area. A path begins here, by a national park notice board, and immediately enters larch-woods rising gently.

After about 20mins the path for the Vallon de Clapouse forks left and crosses a footbridge at 1572m. Once across the bridge the trail twists amongst dense vegetation, but soon becomes more open with views upvalley. The hillside up which the path works its way has several fingers of woodland, and after going through one of these you emerge to a view to the head of the valley: to the Col de l'Ailefroide and the ridge rising to L'Ailefroide itself, with remnant glaciers looking clean against a rocky backdrop. Then the trail contours before entering the next woodland finger.

After about 1hr the gradient steepens with numerous zigzags, taking you up to where the hillside is carpeted with alpenroses and to views north to Mont Pelvoux, its glacier like an icy crown. The way twists up the left-hand side of the waterfall noted above, before slanting away left then right in long loops, passing along the edge of a lovely meadow-like dome giving a bird's-eye view down to Ailefroide. A few minutes later you emerge at the entrance to the Vallon de Clapouse and the larch-topped bluff seen from Ailefroide – the **Bosse de Clapouse**.

Ahead the hanging valley is filled with a desolation of scree and rock tips, practically without vegetation. Pockets of old winter snow lie for much of the summer; otherwise the scene is all but devoid of colour. Until you gaze into the Vallon de la Sélé, that is, or across to Mont Pelvoux, or, best of all, to the northeast where a towering, multi-faceted wall soars above and behind Ailefroide with a crest of aiguilles jutting from it. The site is a near-perfect one for a picnic.

Returning to Ailefroide by the same path will take about 1½hrs.

Route 34: Ailefroide (1507m) –
Refuge du Pelvoux (2704m)

Grade:	2–3
Distance:	7 kilometres (one way)
Height gain:	1197 metres
Time:	3½–4hrs (6½hrs round trip)
Location:	West of Ailefroide

Refuge du Pelvoux, a well-appointed, stone-built hut, is located on a rock shelf high above the Vallon de la Sélé, on the south slopes of Mont Pelvoux. The approach walk, though long, is not difficult and is therefore popular with walkers as well as mountaineers bound for higher routes.

Follow directions into the Vallon de la Sélé as per Route 33, but when the path for the Vallon de Clapouse breaks left after 20mins, continue ahead, remaining on the right-hand side of the Celse Nière torrent. The valley curves to the right, while a fine waterfall can be seen spraying from the Vallon de Clapouse to the left. After 40mins or so you emerge from the woods to a more rugged scene, with the valley stretching ahead. Wild raspberries and clumps of bilberry and juniper clamber over rocks beside the trail. Although Mont Pelvoux forms the right-hand wall of the valley, there is no suggestion as yet that big mountains are so close. Gaining height in easy zigzags Refuge du Sélé may be detected on a prominent rock shoulder towards the head of the valley.

About 1½hrs from Ailefroide come to a junction of paths at 1993m and turn right (sign for Refuge du Pelvoux, 2hrs). The trail angles to a corner, then cuts back left and twists in loops up the hillside, which becomes increasingly wild as height is gained, keeping well to the left of the Prouvarel ravine. Looking up, the way is confused by a series of rock bands; in fact the refuge is not seen at all until moments before it is reached. But the way eventually rakes well to the left (a large cairn should be detected above), then a final pull brings you to the cairn and the **Refuge du Pelvoux** (2704m: *accommodation, refreshments*), which sits just behind it.

The refuge has a lofty outlook, with the Queyras mountains seen far off beyond the east wall of the Vallée de la Vallouise. Formerly known as the Refuge Lemercier, after the president of the CAF in 1891–92, the renovated hut was inaugurated in 1963 by Maurice Herzog, who at the time was Minister of Youth and Sport, but better known as leader of the expedition that made the first ascent of Annapurna in 1950.

Route 35: Ailefroide (1507m) – Refuge du Sélé (2511m)

Grade:	3
Distance:	7 kilometres (one way)
Height gain:	1004 metres
Time:	3hrs (5hrs round trip)
Location:	Southwest of Ailefroide

Whilst the site of the Sélé refuge near the head of the Vallon de la Sélé is unarguably impressive, and the route to it an entertaining one, the hut itself must vie for the title of ugliest building in the Alps! Be that as it may, it's a comfortable, welcoming place, whose approach provides a memorable day out. However, none should attempt this route if they suffer from vertigo, for the crux is the ascent of a steep rock barrier aided by a series of long fixed cables – not unduly difficult for mountain walkers with some scrambling experience, but serious enough to deter the unprepared.

Leaving Ailefroide wander through the Vallon de la Sélé as far as the fork where the path to Refuge du Pelvoux breaks off to the right (1993m, 1½hrs – Routes 33 and 34). Continue ahead, making height without too much effort. To the west the valley closes in, with rock walls on three sides and a hanging glacier glimpsed above to the right. On reaching an upper level, huge boulders and rocks lie in disarray, while the Torrent de Celse Nière, which bursts from a cleft at the left-hand end of the rock wall ahead, flows creamy-grey to betray its glacial origins.

Cairns and white paint marks guide the way to the base of the rock wall at a point to the right of the waterfall. Here the route begins its zigzag ascent with the aid of numerous fixed ropes and cables. Some sections are very exposed and potentially dangerous, and caution should be adopted at all times. At the top of the fixed ropes/cables the way twists up a little higher, then contours through a gap towards the true head of the valley – a grim scene of ochre rock walls, glaciers, screes, moraines and a wilderness seemingly devoid of vegetation.

Come to a path junction (not very prominent) with the letters REF painted in red on a rock, indicating the way up to the refuge. Turning to the right you'll see it above and almost behind you. From here a stony path twists up the final slope to gain the **Refuge du Sélé** (2511m: *accommodation, refreshments*).

This is the third such hut built in the vicinity, the first two being abandoned through danger of avalanche. The present bunker-style refuge was built in 1983, and is owned by the Briançon section of the Club Alpin Français. Set on the flat top of the rock barrier, views downvalley are unrestricted, with the Pelvoux refuge clearly seen to the northeast. Looking west the view to the head of the valley is likewise unrestricted, and shows the glacial-carved cirque in all its barren splendour. The cirque is formed by the curving ridges of L'Ailefroide, Cime du Coin, Pointe du Sélé and the Crête de Boeufs Rouges, and just below Pointe du Sélé the glacial Col du Sélé shows the easiest way over the headwall. On the far side of that headwall lies the Glacier de la Pilatte, which spills into the upper Vallée du Vénéon above La Bérarde.

Route 36: Ailefroide (1507m) – Pré de Madame Carle (Refuge Cézanne) (1874m)

Grade:	1
Distance:	5 kilometres (one way)
Height gain:	367 metres
Time:	1½hrs (2½hrs round trip)
Location:	North of Ailefroide

'The scenery of the Vallon d'Ailefroide, as this arm of the Vallouise is called, is exceedingly fine, the tremendous cliffs of the Pelvoux on the right [west] side being objects of extraordinary grandeur.' So wrote A.W. Moore in **The Alps in 1864***. What was true in the 19th century is still true in the 21st, and at the head of this valley the stony plain of Pré de Madame Carle, which lies at the foot of the Glaciers Noir and Blanc, is the starting point for two highly recommended walks and numerous climbs. There's a large car park, also served daily in summer by bus from Vallouise and Ailefroide, but as an alternative to the road journey this walk makes an enjoyable way of getting there. Keeping company with the St Pierre river for much of the way, the route winds among trees and through patches of juniper, bilberry and wild raspberry, with only brief contact with the road.*

Walking out of Ailefroide village heading north you soon come to the last of the camping areas. This is found on the right side of the road at the foot of the great cliffs that are so popular with climbers. A path cuts along the left-hand side of the road here, between it and the river, and takes you a short distance before veering onto the road again. For the first kilometre or two there will be a succession of loosely connected trails (no signposts or waymarks) dodging from the tarmac only to rejoin it after a short distance, but when the road starts to climb in easy hairpins the path crosses and recrosses, and becomes a clear route. It's a very pleasant path too.

Near the head of the valley a sign announces the Réserve Naturelle de Torrent de Saint Pierre, with the trail ducking behind the sign. At the top of the hairpins mount a high bluff carpeted with bilberries, from where you gain a splendid view of the plain ahead, with the Glacier Blanc curving down towards the ice-smoothed cliffs that effectively block that upper part of the valley.

Over the bluff descend to the road and cross the river by bridge. From here to Refuge Cézanne there are vague traces of path on the left of the road (the river is now on the right), but it's probably easier to remain on the road itself for this final stretch. So come to the huge parking area, at the northern end of which stands a national park information centre, and **Refuge Cézanne** (also known as Chalet-Refuge du Pré de Madame Carle) (1874m: *accommodation, refreshments*).

'There were no signs of vegetation, nothing on all sides but stones and sand,' wrote Moore when he arrived here after dark, having made the first ascent of the Barre des Écrins with Whymper. 'Although we could not see, we knew that we were in the middle of a flat plain, perfectly barren and desolate, which lies below the termination of the Glaciers Noir and Blanc.' Routes that provide close views of those glaciers are given below.

Route 37: Pré de Madame Carle (1874m) – Glacier Noir (2510m)

Grade:	2
Distance:	4 kilometres (one way)
Height gain:	636 metres
Time:	1½–2hrs (3–3¼hrs round trip)
Location:	West of Pré de Madame Carle

Of the two glaciers that drain into the Pré de Madame Carle basin, Glacier Noir ('the black glacier') is the easier of access, since its moraine walls are seen pushing towards the northern edge of the plain from the left. The path taken by this walk mounts the north lateral moraine, which gives such a dramatic view onto and across the glacier. As to the 'noir' of its name, this refers to its covering of dark rock debris, which is in direct contrast to the cleaner snow cover of Glacier Blanc. Whilst this walk is not difficult, a warning is given that the moraine wall is steep, narrow and, in places, liable to crumble, so care should be taken at all times.

From the roadhead a broad path strikes ahead among larches between Refuge Cézanne and the national park information centre, where a sign gives 1½hrs for the Glacier Noir. Cross a side-stream and pass among alders to a second bridge, this one crossing the torrent from Glacier Noir, whose impressive lateral moraine is such a feature of the view. A broad path, partially paved, now swings left and begins a zigzag ascent of the mountainside west of the slabs that were polished long ago by the Glacier Blanc.

After 30mins come to a signed junction and bear left (the right-hand path is the one to take for Refuge Glacier Blanc). Very soon the path brings you onto the crest of the moraine wall, and the walk simply follows this crest almost to its upper end, maintaining a steady gradient throughout. The highest point reached by most people is a large cairn at about 2445m (it has a memorial plate). Views are very fine, if bleak and almost monochrome, with the massive walls of Mont Pelvoux, Pic Sans Nom and L'Ailefroide soaring above the far side of the glacier.

Beyond the cairn the moraine dips, then rises again before terminating among rocks and screes coming from the Barre des Écrins above the final cirque wall. About 10mins will see you to the farthest point at around 2510m – but take especial care as the moraine crest is narrow and liable to crumble in places. This farthest point should appeal to all who love wild Alpine scenery, for the panorama of rugged mountain architecture adorned with hanging glaciers, screes, moraines and rubble-covered ice is powerful, menacing, yet beautiful in a savage way.

Route 38: Pré de Madame Carle (1874m) – Refuge du Glacier Blanc (2543m)

Grade:	3
Distance:	4 kilometres (one way)
Height gain:	669 metres
Time:	2–2¼hrs (4hrs round trip)
Location:	North of Pré de Madame Carle

Not surprisingly the Glacier Blanc refuge is one of the most visited in the Écrins region, with excellent close views of the Glacier Blanc icefall and a more distant outlook to the multi-peaked Mont Pelvoux. The first part of the walk is by way of a steeply twisting path leading to a boulder-scape below the glacier, while the upper section is tougher, calls for a little scrambling and negotiates one short slab safeguarded with iron rungs; both sections demand a certain amount of agility. If you're intimidated by prospects of the upper stage of the walk, aim only as far as the boulderscape below the glacier, where the scenery is quite magnificent, albeit not quite as dramatic as from the refuge.

From the roadhead car park walk ahead following directions as for Route 37 as far as the path junction (30mins) where the way to Glacier Noir breaks left. The invariably busy main path heads to the right and gains height with numerous zigzags in order to surmount the great glacial slabs that from below appear to support the Glacier Blanc. It will take about 1–1¼hrs to reach the vantage point (2288m) amongst the ice-smoothed boulders, with the tongue of the cascading glacier directly ahead. The refuge can be seen about 250m above, just to the right of the icefall.

The path slopes down to cross a footbridge over the glacial torrent, then swings left towards the glacier before cutting to the right up grit-covered ledges and slabs, the way marked with red stripes and arrows. Coming to a level area, note the sign indicating 'museum' 50m to the right. This refers to the former Refuge Tuckett, a small stone-built hut from which there's a splendid view of Mont Pelvoux.

Pass to the left of the Tuckett refuge alongside a small tarn, then snake up to the rocky bluff on which the Glacier Blanc hut rests. Take care when climbing the iron rungs that aid the ascent of a slab, and a little higher you have a metal handrail to use should the rocks be slippery. The path then eases and cuts back to the right to approach **Refuge du Glacier Blanc** (2543m: *accommodation, refreshments*) by the 'back door'.

VALGAUDEMAR

Picturesque groups of stone-walled houses lie dotted through the valley, becoming more and more scarce towards its head, where the Valgaudemar takes on a challenging aspect. The valley penetrates deeper into the heart of the mountains than any other tributary of the Drac, and upstream of Villar-Loubière it has an ambience all its own: warm yet uncompromising, its vegetation tangled but colourful. Under brooding skies the valley may seem oppressive, but in sunshine cascades sparkle and numerous rivers stream from the heights.

ACCESS AND INFORMATION

Location: West of the Vallée de la Vallouise, the Valgaudemar projects deeply into the heart of the Parc National des Écrins, south of the Olan massif

Bases: La Chapelle-en-Valgaudemar (1100m)

Information: Syndicat d'Initiative, 05800 La Chapelle-en-Valgaudemar (☎ 04 92 55 23 21)

Maison du Parc, 05800 La Chapelle-en-Valgaudemar (☎ 04 92 55 25 19)

Access: By the N85 Grenoble–Gap road, turn east at St Firmin onto D985A, which leads to La Chapelle. Beyond La Chapelle D480 extends for 9km as far as the Chalet-Hôtel du Gioberney. Bus and railway services run between Grenoble and Gap, and local buses to St Firmin and La Chapelle.

INTRODUCTION

The valley of the Séveraisse torrent has cut a deep trench into the Écrins mountains. Rising among the glaciers of Le Sirac, Pointe de Verdonne and Pic de Bonvoisin, it rushes northward down to a confluence of streams at the foot of Les Bans (see Appendix B), then curves sharply to the west. Here its banks are tangled with trees and shrubs, the valley walls are steep and constricting and all-but glacier-free, and waterfalls ribbon their flanks. One or two tiny huddles of stone houses are the only habitation until La Chapelle is reached. Though small, it makes an important centre, while the northern hillsides are sprinkled with mountain huts. Behind the village to the south a minor road snakes up to Les Portes, a tiny hamlet full of simple charm in the Vallon de Navette. Nearby a stone-built hump-backed bridge spans the torrent over the potholes of the Oulles du Diable.

Below La Chapelle the Séveraisse loops round Les Andrieux, which huddles in the shadow of the 2653m Aiguille du Midi des Andrieux, then begins to curve southwest at Villar-Loubière. This village is visited by the Tour de l'Oisans, whose route leaves the valley at this point by cutting north into a narrow gorge-like glen at the base of Pic des Souffles, and crossing out of it by way of Col de Vaurze. Meanwhile, moving downstream from Villar-Loubière in the Valgaudemar, an eastward view shows the village as a lovely foreground to the heights of Les Bans and Pic de Bonvoisin, with the Glacier des Aupillous hanging between them.

The lower valley, between Villar-Loubière and St Firmin, is softened with pastures lined with poplars. The main road keeps to the right bank of the river and is narrow and twisting, while a secondary road links three hamlets on the left (south) bank. When you turn back for a view upstream, L'Olan (3564m) (see Appendix B) rises like a great rock pyramid on the north wall of the valley.

Thanks to the severe nature of the upper valley, Valgaudemar is exposed to winter avalanche and has therefore escaped the attention of the downhill ski enthusiast. This absence of mechanical aids only increases the valley's appeal in summer, a lure that's hard to resist.

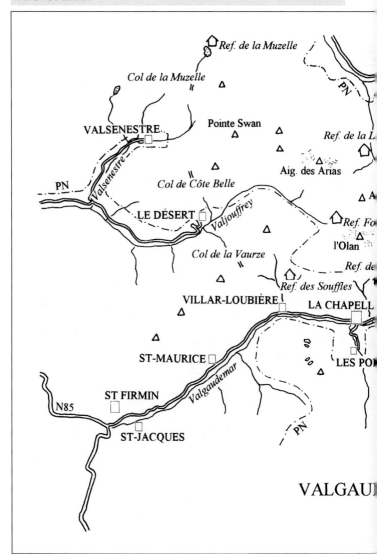

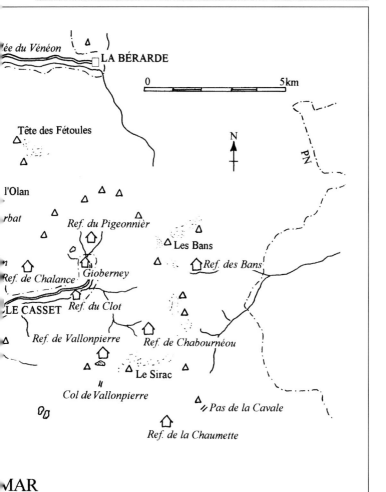

ée du Vénéon
LA BÉRARDE

0   5km

Tête des Fétoules

l'Olan

rbat

Ref. du Pigeonnièr

Les Bans

Ref. des Bans

n

Ref. de Chalance   *Gioberney*

LE CASSET   *Ref. du Clot*

Ref. de Vallonpierre   *Ref. de Chabournéou*

Le Sirac

Col de Vallonpierre

Pas de la Cavale

Ref. de la Chaumette

MAR

N

PN

MAIN VALLEY BASE

- **LA CHAPELLE-EN-VALGAUDEMAR** (1100m) is little more than a modest village, but with enough facilities to make it a reasonable base for a walking holiday. It has a hotel, two *gîtes d'étape* (Mairie, 47 places: ☎ 04 92 55 23 17, and Foyer Rural, 28 places: ☎ 04 92 55 28 56) and a campsite, PTT, shops and restaurants. There's a tourist office, Bureau des Guides and a national park information office (Maison du Parc).

OTHER VALLEY BASES

At the roadhead 9km upvalley from La Chapelle, and in a splendid location, the large renovated **CHALET-HÔTEL DU GIOBERNEY** marks the start of several walks. Owned by the local community it has 90 beds and dormitory options (☎ 04 92 55 27 50). Elsewhere in the Valgaudemar there are *gîtes* at **LE CASSET** (18 places: ☎ 04 92 55 22 72), two in **VILLAR-LOUBIÈRE** (Le Relais de la Vaurze: ☎ 04 92 55 23 61 and La Charrière: ☎ 04 92 55 24 18), and one each in the lower valley at **ST-MAURICE-EN-VALGODEMARD** (Les Barrengeards: ☎ 04 92 55 23 75) and **ST-JACQUES-EN-VALGO-DEMARD** (Les Paris: ☎ 04 92 55 30 07).

MOUNTAIN HUTS

No less than seven refuges are accessible from the valley, and are detailed below. As elsewhere in the Écrins region it is essential to book a place in advance should you intend to stay the night.

- **REFUGE DE VALLONPIERRE** (2280m) sits on the north shore of the little Lac de Vallonpierre below the col of the same name, with Le Sirac standing over it to the southeast. Reached by a steep walk of about 3hrs from the head of the valley, it is a small hut of mottled stone owned by the Gap section of the CAF; it has 32 places and a guardian in summer (☎ 04 92 55 27 81).

- **REFUGE DE CHABOURNÉOU** (2050m) is linked with Ref. de Vallonpierre by a trail (2hrs) which cuts across the flank of Le

Sirac. The direct approach from the valley is a little longer, and takes about 2¼hrs. This timber-built hut is also in the care of the Gap section of the CAF, has 60 places and a guardian in winter and summer (☎ 04 92 55 27 80).

- **REFUGE DU PIGEONNIER** (2400m) is located at the head of the valley, as the above two huts, but on the north flank above the Gioberney chalet-hôtel. Another CAF refuge, reached in about 2hrs from the road, there are 60 places and a guardian in summer and winter (☎ 04 92 55 27 82).

- **REFUGE DU CLOT** (1398m), formerly known as Xavier-Blanc, is a very pleasant valley hut set just below the road on the right bank of the Séveraisse stream. CAF-owned, it has places for 40 and is wardened in summer (☎ 04 92 55 27 90).

- **REFUGE DE CHALANCE** (2548m) is a simple, unmanned bivouac hut with places for 11, reached by an approach walk of about 3hrs from the road at Rif du Sap. For bookings, telephone the guardian at Refuge du Clot (☎ 04 92 55 27 90).

- **REFUGE DE L'OLAN** (2345m) is located in a cirque below the 3564m Olan, and is reached in about 3–3½hrs from La Chapelle. Owned by the CAF (section Gap), it has 54 places and a guardian in summer (☎ 04 92 55 30 88).

- **REFUGE DES SOUFFLES** (1968m) is set some 900m above Villar-Loubière on the east side of a corrie dominated by Pic des Souffles. Visited by walkers on GR54, this small hut has just 20 places and is wardened in summer (☎ 04 92 55 2291).

Route 39: Refuge du Pré de la Chaumette (1790m) – Refuge de Vallonpierre (2280m)

Grade:	3
Distance:	14 kilometres
Height gain:	1253 metres
Height loss:	763 metres
Time:	4½–5hrs
Location:	Southeast of La Chapelle – GR54 link route from Vallée du Drac de Champoléon to Valgaudemar

This energetic route, used by the Tour de l'Oisans, crosses three cols in order to skirt the big block of Le Sirac, which dominates the high country between these two huts. First is the highest, Col de la Vallette (2668m), second the Col de Gouiran (2597m), followed by Col de Vallonpierre (2607m). The easiest of the three is Col de Gouiran, while descent from the other two is very steep and demands care in places, especially in wet conditions or in the event of any snow remaining in the early summer. That being said, it's a very fine trekking stage, usually extended as far as La Chapelle-en-Gaudemar, but a night at the Vallonpierre hut is highly recommended.

The path begins by cutting into the little corrie behind Refuge du Pré de la Chaumette heading north towards the mountain wall linking Pointe de Verdonne and Le Sirac. Keeping on the left-hand side of the valley, the way rises through rock-cluttered pastures before curving west round the Puy de la Chaumette and gaining height in long zigzags. Col de la Vallette is seen almost an hour before it's reached, and on the final approach the path steepens; in places it is necessary to use both hands and feet on scrambly pitches and narrow ledges – quite safe, but demanding extra care.

Col de la Vallette is gained in 2–2½hrs, and from it the path to Col de Gouiran can be seen rising out of the green pasture lying below to the northwest. The initial descent requires care as the slope is very steep and the path narrow, but as you lose height so the way improves, and the grassland of the Vallon de Gouiran between the two cols is soon reached. A small pool lies in the midst of the pasture, and the view left (south) gives a hint of the Vallée du Drac de Champoléon far below.

The continuing path leads to the next col in less than an hour after leaving the first, and does so without undue exertion. Col de Gouiran is a bare, windswept saddle overlooking a rust-brown landscape of scree and grit and big bald mountains. Although longer, the descent from this col is easier than from the Vallette, and it cuts round the head of a glen below the western end of Le Sirac's ridge, losing about 250m of altitude before crossing eroded ribs on the way up to Col de Vallonpierre.

Col de Vallonpierre (2607m) crosses at an extremely narrow part of the ridge between Aiguille de Morges and Le Sirac, providing a wonderful point of view. However, the path down on the north side is thin in places and steep too, but with a little attention it should not cause any undue problems and, as with the descent from Col de la Vallette, the way improves with loss of height. If anything, the views become even better too, with a contrast of green hillsides creating a foreground to a panorama of distant mountains wearing snow. Then you turn a spur and look directly down on the milky-blue Lac and **Refuge de Vallonpierre** (2280m: *accommodation, refreshments*), which is reached shortly after.

Route 40: Refuge de Vallonpierre (2280m) – La Chapelle-en-Valgaudemar (1100m)

Grade:	**2**
Distance:	**11 kilometres**
Height loss:	**1180 metres**
Time:	**4hrs**
Location:	**Southeast of La Chapelle**

This is the continuation of the GR54 (Tour de l'Oisans) crossing from Refuge du Pré de la Chaumette, a delightful descent that can be properly enjoyed following a night at Vallonpierre, rather than experienced as a foot-weary descent in a very long day's walking. The scenery is outstanding almost all the way.

Out of the Vallonpierre refuge turn left and wander across to the main path which swings left (north) among rocks, passes a small stone hut and descends a hillside clothed with alpenroses. The path

Rufuge du Clot, otherwise known as Refuge Xavier-Blanc, romantically set on the bank of the Severaisse, near the head of the Valgaudemar (Routes 40, 41)

steepens and twists in zigzags, and at the foot of these you have a fine view to the right into a cirque topped by Pointe de Chabournéou, Pointe de Verdonne and Pointe de Queyre. In that cirque (unseen from here) stands Refuge de Chabournéou, which may be reached by a trail from the Vallonpierre hut.

Streams drain out of that cirque to form the Séveraisse, and the path wanders down through meadows alongside it. About 2hrs from Vallonpierre the path, which has been led by drystone walls for a while, crosses the Séveraisse to its right bank and, winding among huge boulders and trees, comes to **Refuge du Clot/Xavier-Blanc** (1398m: *accommodation, refreshments*).

Continue along the path which forks about 5mins beyond the refuge. Take the left-hand option which is a pleasant waymarked trail fighting a way through luxuriant vegetation. Pass the few buildings of Rif du Sap and continue on the right bank of the river. The path becomes a track which leads to a spur of road opposite Le Bourg. Cross the bridge to the 'lost-world' hamlet of Le Bourg, and turn right on the continuing path. Remaining on the left bank eventually come to another bridge across the river. This leads to **Le Casset** (1151m: *accommodation, refreshments*), which has a *gîte d'étape*. Unless you plan to spend the night there, continue on the left bank all the way to **La Chapelle-en-Valgaudemar** (1100m: *accommodation, refreshments*).

Route 41: Refuge du Clot (1398m) – Refuge de Vallonpierre (2280m)

Grade:	2
Distance:	5½ kilometres (one way)
Height gain:	882 metres
Time:	3hrs
Location:	East and southeast of La Chapelle

Although Refuge de Vallonpierre is visited during the multi-day linking of the Vallée de la Vallouise with Valgaudemar (Routes 25, 39, 40), it is included here as a way of drawing the attention of Valgaudemar-based walkers to the rather splendid setting of this hut. The walk to it is steep at times, but it's a scenic route with much to commend it. As for Refuge du Clot (or Xavier-Blanc), this can be reached by riverside footpath from La Chapelle in about 2hrs. Walkers with their own transport should drive about 7km upvalley from La Chapelle to where the road widens as the hut's parking area. From it a track slopes down towards the river, and a little over 5mins later you reach the Refuge du Clot.

Turn left on leaving the hut and follow a good path upstream for about 15mins, where you cross a bridge to the south bank. Before long the way goes alongside and through a large meadow heading roughly south towards Le Sirac, with its ragged crest above a drape of little glaciers looking impressive ahead. The way steepens as the valley narrows, and on coming to a path junction (30mins from Ref. du Clot) the GR54 continues ahead. In another 15mins cross a bridge over a side-stream, and a little after this cross another to the right-hand side of the Séveraisse.

For a while you wander through another fairly level meadowland before starting to climb. At about 1648m pass a national park warden's hut, after which you come to another path junction (signpost). The right-hand option is the way to Vallonpierre, and it climbs on with good views left into the Chabournéou cirque. A footbridge takes you across another side-stream, followed by a steep climb with numerous zigzags that eventually brings you into a rock-strewn meadow with the **Refuge de Vallonpierre** (2280m: *accommodation, refreshments*) off to the right.

Route 42: Refuge de Vallonpierre (2280m) – Refuge de Chabournéou (2050m)

Grade:	2–3
Distance:	4 kilometres (one way)
Height loss:	230 metres
Time:	2hrs
Location:	Northeast of Refuge de Vallonpierre

Note that this route, which makes a traverse below the North Face of Le Sirac, could be potentially dangerous in bad weather or following heavy rainfall. For up-to-date advice, consult the guardian at the Vallonpierre hut.

Out of the refuge turn left, and in the meadow east of the tarn a trail junction bears a sign directing the route to the Chabournéou refuge. This cuts northeast to turn the spur of the Banc des Aiguilles, picking a way round the steep slopes then closing under the Sirac glacier. This is an impressive contour, but you should keep alert for any possibility of stonefall. The trail is clearly marked, narrow and a little exposed in places, and it leads directly to the **Refuge de Chabournéou** (2050m: *accommodation, refreshments*), set on a grassy shelf with a good close view of Le Sirac and its glaciers. A direct descent to the Valgaudemar can be made in about 1½hrs. There's also a longer alternative route via the Gioberney chalet-hôtel.

Route 43: Chalet-Hôtel du Gioberney (1642m) – Lac du Lauzon (2008m) – Chalet-Hôtel du Gioberney

Grade:	2
Distance:	5 kilometres
Height gain/loss:	428 metres
Time:	2–2¼hrs
Location:	Northeast of La Chapelle

With its very fine panoramic view of the glacial cirque which closes off the head of the valley, Lac du Lauzon makes an understandably popular destination for a walk. The route is neither long nor difficult, and is well signed from the roadhead.

The trail begins behind the chalet-hôtel (signpost) and at first heads north before breaking left (west and south) to climb in fairly moderate zigzags up the hillside. After about half an hour a footbridge takes the path across a stream, and continues to rise in order to gain a meadowland and another stream near a whole series of cascades spraying down a rock wall. A few minutes later you top a rise with the **Lac du Lauzon** just ahead (1hr). The view from here encompasses a dramatic sweep of mountains curving in a waterfall-streaked amphitheatre; Le Sirac is often reflected in the water.

Continue north of the tarn, rising again to about 2070m before descending to a path junction at 2020m, 20mins from Lac du Lauzon. The left-hand option goes to Refuge du Pigeonnier (Route 44), while we bear right and descend to the **Gioberney chalet-hôtel**.

Route 44: Chalet-Hôtel du Gioberney (1642m) – Refuge du Pigeonnier (2400m)

Grade:	2–3
Distance:	2½ kilometres (one way)
Height gain:	758 metres
Time:	2¼hrs
Location:	Northeast of La Chapelle

This is one of several hut walks accessible from the head of the valley, Refuge du Pigeonnier being located north of the chalet-hôtel, on a shoulder below the Crête de l'Orient, dividing the valleys of Muande and Gioberney.

Head north behind the Chalet-Hôtel du Gioberney to wander up the valley of the Muande Bellone torrent, continuing ahead when the path to Lac du Lauzon (Route 43) breaks away to the left. Soon after this the path twists left in zigzags to avoid a rockband, then swings north again along terraces before rising to another junction. Take the right fork over the stream – this is often achieved on a snow bridge; otherwise use stepping stones.

The way now zigzags to gain more height, and on coming to another stream keep this to your right. The gradient steepens as you climb north, then east, and cross the stream near a waterfall at about 2160m (30mins from the path junction). Keep rising in zigzags again towards an obvious rock slab. Passing this to your left, the trail is somewhat exposed and caution is advised. In another 10mins or so you reach the **Refuge du Pigeonnier** (2400m: *accommodation, refreshments*).

Allow 2hrs for the descent to Gioberney by the same route.

Route 45: La Chapelle-en-Valgaudemar (1100m) – Refuge de l'Olan (2345m)

Grade:	3
Distance:	4 kilometres (one way)
Height gain:	1245 metres
Time:	3½hrs
Location:	North of La Chapelle

The route to the Olan hut, which was rebuilt in 1979, is almost unrelentingly steep, and in the height of summer it can be an exhaustingly hot walk, so you're advised to make an early start and pace yourself in order to enjoy the ascent as it should be properly appreciated. There's plenty to enjoy.

Start by walking up the main valley road from La Chapelle. About 300m outside the village a sign directs you north (left) into the valley of the Torrent du Clot. The path mounts the east side of this valley in zigzags, cascades showering down the steep mountainsides and the torrent thundering below in its bed. Cross a footbridge below the Cascade de Combefroide (1hr 15mins), and 10 mins later reach a path junction. The Vallon du Clot branches left (northwest) where the alternative path goes to the Col de Colombes, while we fork right, climbing still before crossing the Torrent de Combefroide.

Now on the east side of the torrent the trail zigzags again up slopes of grass and rock. Despite the gradient there's nothing unduly difficult or complicated about the way, and eventually it turns a spur, cuts left with a few cairns, and comes out just above the **Refuge de l'Olan** (2345m: *accommodation, refreshments*), which is tucked against the mountain at the lower edge of the Cros des Levats cirque. L'Olan itself cannot be seen from the hut, which looks south across the Valgaudemar to the Vallon de Navette, cutting behind La Chapelle, but a short walk above it reveals the full extent of the cirque and the great rock peak of L'Olan (3564m) – one of the major peaks of the Écrins region, whose 1000m Northwest Face (undetected from the hut) is a Dauphiné testpiece climb.

Allow 2½hrs for the descent by the same route.

Route 46: La Chapelle-en-Valgaudemar (1100m) – Lacs de Pétarel (2090m)

Grade:	3
Distance:	5½ kilometres (one way)
Height gain:	990 metres
Time:	3½hrs
Location:	Southwest of La Chapelle

The national park boundary makes a kink behind La Chapelle where the Vallon de Navette slices into the mountain wall. The east side of the vallon is included in the park, but a portion of the west flank of the glen is not, for the boundary is traced a short way along the ridge-crest of Pic des Ours. Below this ridge, on its west side, lie two groups of tarns near the head of a hanging valley topped by Pic Pétarel: the Lacs de Cebeyras

and the lower Lacs de Pétarel. This walk visits the lower tarns in a
seemingly remote setting.

Take the path heading south out of La Chapelle on the east bank
of the Navette stream and follow this upvalley to the hamlet of Les
Portes (see 'Other Walks', below), which sits on the west bank. At
the lower (northern) end of the hamlet a sign directs the route to the
lakes, rising through meadows and into the Bois des Blancs – the
woodland that blankets the southern slopes of the Valgaudemar.
Through the woods you emerge to more meadows on a rising
traverse of hillside, and about 2hrs after leaving La Chapelle you
cross a stream which, in fact, flows from the lakes, and come to a
signposted junction of trails.

Turn left and climb among trees, steeply in places, to another
junction, where the right fork is signed to La Muande. We take the
left branch and climb in more zigzags, emerging from the woods
and rising to gain the first of the **Lacs de Pétarel**. The second is set
just a little higher. Allow 2½hrs to return to La Chapelle.

Other Walks from La Chapelle-en-Valgaudemar

A diverse selection of walks is possible from a base at La Chapelle.
Valley walks, both up and downstream, can be rewarding for their
scenic contrasts despite their modest nature, while more
challenging routes lead to high and notable viewpoints.

- Of the easier (and shorter) outings, mention must be made of
  the hour-long there-and-back walk to the hamlet of **LES
  PORTES** and the **OULLES DU DIABLE**, where the Navette
  torrent south of La Chapelle is squeezed furiously through a
  narrow channel (see above). This is an understandably popular
  picnic site.

- From Les Portes a longer, and quite steep, route climbs to the
  belvedere of **LE CHAPEAU** (2372m), high on the east flank of
  the Vallon de Navette. Walkers should allow 3–3½hrs for the
  ascent and 2½hrs for a return by the same path, or take the more
  challenging way down heading northeast to Rif du Sap several
  kilometres upvalley from La Chapelle. Le Chapeau rewards
  with excellent views to L'Olan across the Valgaudemar.

Route 47: Villar-Loubière (1037m) – Refuge des Souffles (1968m)

Grade:	2
Distance:	4 kilometres (one way)
Height gain:	931 metres
Time:	2½hrs
Location:	Northwest of La Chapelle

There are two ways of reaching Refuge des Souffles from the Valgaudemar: the longer route going north from La Chapelle towards the Olan hut, then cutting northwest to Col de Colombes and Col des Clochettes; and the more direct route which follows GR54 from Villar-Loubière. This is the walk described here. Thanks to the GR54 it's a well-marked, well-trodden route that will rarely be walked in solitude.

From Villar-Loubière the waymarked path is clearly evident, leading from a minor service road north of the main valley road. On leaving the village the way mounts the right-hand side of a ravine cut by the Villar torrent draining out of a grassy cirque overlooked by Pic des Souffles, and as you progress through it, so the path twists in zigzags with views opening as height is gained. Ignore alternative paths and stick to the main waymarked route until you're almost at the hut. A slight diversion to the right away from GR54 brings you to the flat-roofed **Refuge des Souffles** (1968m: *accommodation, refreshments*), which faces south from its vegetated 'nest'. Descent to Villar-Loubière by the same route will take about 1½hrs.

Route 48: Villar-Loubière (1037m) – Col de la Vaurze (2500m) – Le Désert (1266m)

Grade:	3
Distance:	13 kilometres
Height gain:	1463 metres
Height loss:	1234 metres
Time:	7–7½hrs
Location:	Northwest of La Chapelle

The Tour de l'Oisans turns roughly northward out of the Valgaudemar on what are usually seen as the final three or four stages to Bourg d'Oisans. The first of these stages crosses the mountains spreading west and southwest of L'Olan to the sparsely inhabited Valjouffrey, the upper valley of the River Bonne whose lower reaches are known as the Valbonnais. It makes a fine, if demanding, day's trek, while accommodation is available in the little village of Le Désert at the end of the day.

Follow directions given under Route 47 as far as the path junction a little west of the **Refuge des Souffles** (1968m, 2½hrs: *accommodation, refreshments*). Instead of turning off here GR54 swings northwest without gaining much height in a lengthy traverse round the great pastoral cirque below Pic des Souffles. Across this amphitheatre, roughly west of the hut, the path then rises in long sweeping zigzags towards the saddle of Col de la Vaorze. Here and there alpenroses colour the hillside, in places alder thickets bully the way; almost always fine views accompany the walk.

Col de la Vaorze (2500m) is reached about 4hrs 45mins after leaving Villar-Loubière, and it is a wonderful place to relax for a while and absorb the extensive panorama which includes La Chapelle far below to the southeast, Le Sirac above and beyond the village, and the big block of L'Olan which dominates the view to the east. On the north side of the col, Le Désert – though more than 1200m below – looks surprisingly close, and above that the notch of the Col de Côte Belle marks the crux of the next stage of the tour.

Descent to the Valjouffrey is straightforward, but very steep and tiring, and with the village in view virtually the whole time. Once down, **Le Désert** (1266m: *accommodation, refreshments*) is a small but attractively rural village with barns crowding its street, which help give it plenty of atmosphere. It offers accommodation in a *gîte d'étape* (30 places: ☎ 04 76 30 27 01) and a *gîte de séjour* (18 places: ☎ 04 76 30 21 45), and has a foodstore and a bar. (The continuing GR54 route to Valsenestre is described below as Route 49.)

Notes on the Valjouffrey

Upstream of Le Désert (or to be precise, Le Désert-en-Valjouffrey) the valley has clearly been carved by glacial action. At its head rise the impressive North and Northwest Faces of L'Olan and the

Aiguille de l'Olan, which together form the cirque in which sits the remote **Refuge de Fond Turbat** (2194m, 30 places: ☎ 04 76 80 22 93). This hut is reached by a walk of about 3–3½hrs from Le Désert, a walk which passes the notable Cascade de la Pisse on the national park boundary.

As noted at the start of Route 48, Valjouffrey is the upper valley of the Bonne torrent which, lower down, is known as the Valbonnais. Like the Valgaudemar, this also pushes deep into the Écrins region, its outlet being the little township of La Mure. This is served by both bus and train from Grenoble, and from La Mure buses go upvalley as far as Entraigues (14km from Le Désert), from which the D526 road continues north to the Romanche a short distance from Bourg d'Oisans.

Route 49: Le Désert (1266m) – Col de Côte Belle (2290m) – Valsenestre (1294m)

Grade:	3
Distance:	9 kilometres
Height gain:	1024 metres
Height loss:	996 metres
Time:	4½–5hrs
Location:	North of Le Désert

Col de Côte Belle provides an obvious crossing point in the block of mountains which divides the two upper stems of the Valbonnais. While it is the Bonne torrent which drains the Valjouffrey, it is the Béranger that flows through the Valsenestre, with the confluence of these two streams being guarded by La Chapelle-en-Valjouffrey about 7km downstream from Le Désert. Anyone with a schedule to keep and faced by bad weather for this stage of the Tour de l'Oisans could thereby opt for a valley route between the two villages. But that would be a shame because the crossing of Col de Côte Belle is another enjoyable mountain day.

On leaving Le Désert walk upvalley a short way on a road which becomes a track, then a path which turns north into the grassy ravine leading to the col. The way soon crosses to the right-hand side of the stream (the Ruisseau de la Laisse) and rises among feathery grasses intermingled with flowers. It's another straightforward ascent without difficulty, and the col, which is a broad grassy saddle enjoying more fine views both ahead and behind, is gained about 2¼–2½hrs after setting out.

The way down is steep at times, but always interesting. In one place the path squeezes between spiky, shattered slate-like formations; lower down the hillside is like a wild Alpine garden. Dwarf growths of silver birch brighten the way, and towards the base of the mountain there are forests of larch, pine and fir. Down in the valley the path forks. One option is for the Col de la Muzelle (for the GR54 stage to Bourg d'Arud), while the path to Valsenestre swings left along a forest track.

Valsenestre (1294m: *accommodation, refreshments*), which is only occupied in summer, has accommodation in a *gîte de séjour* (24 places: ☎ 04 76 30 20 88) which also provides drinks and snacks, café style. The hamlet has been prettily 'gentrified' with several of its buildings being taken over as holiday homes. Once a much larger community than it is today, the *gîte* was formerly the village school. (The next stage of the Tour de l'Oisans, which crosses the mountains to Bourg d'Arud, is described below as Route 50.)

Notes on the Valsenestre

The Béranger tributary of the Bonne, which runs through the Valsenestre glen, is much shorter than the Valjouffrey stem of the valley. Entering from La Chapelle-en-Valjouffrey the D117a road snakes through the Gorges du Béranger in a *réserve naturelle*, then along wooded slopes before crossing the Pont Moulin to enter **Valsenestre** village. The valley ends a short distance to the east, where Pointe Swan looks down into it as just one of many high points in a swastika-shaped ridge system that walls and contains several glens. North of the village a path climbs through a minor glen to the Cabane du Vallon; south of the village another snakes up to Pic de Valsenestre, while a variation of GR54 goes northwest then north to Col de la Romeiou and Brêche du Périer on the way to La Danchère near Venosc. Halfway along this latter route a fork in the trail sends another path southwest to the village of Le Périer (*gîtes d'étape*), which lies on the D526 upvalley of Entraigues on the way to the Romanche. Valsenestre, then, provides a variety of options for other walks and long treks. Study the map for ideas.

Route 50: Valsenestre (1294m) – Col de la Muzelle (2625m) – Bourg d'Arud (942m)

Grade:	3
Distance:	16 kilometres
Height gain:	1331 metres
Height loss:	1683 metres
Time:	7½hrs
Location:	Northeast of Valsenestre

Usually tackled as the penultimate stage of the Tour de l'Oisans, this long day's trek could be broken by an overnight in Refuge de la Muzelle on the north side of the col, although in good conditions the full descent to the Vallée du Vénéon should be acceptable.

Wander upvalley from Valsenestre to the path junction where GR54 breaks south to Col de Côte Belle and north to Col de la Muzelle. The waymarked path leading to Col de la Muzelle mounts through a ravine-like glen, soon crossing to the left-hand side of the stream and climbing in zigzags. Mostly this is a reasonable trail that, in its upper section, is shown on the map (and described in both English and French guides) as being either difficult or hazardous. That it may be in wet or snowy conditions, but when dry it should cause no undue concern. This particular section consists of a long, steep cone of black shale and grit taking about 45mins to climb. There is a narrow path, and a trekking pole would be useful under less than perfect conditions. It leads directly onto the **col** about 3½hrs after leaving Valsenestre.

The col is another crossing with a scenic outlook. The view south, back the way you've come, shows both Col de Côte Belle and Col de la Vaorze; below to the north lies the green Lac de la Muzelle in a pastureland. In the middle distance are seen the skilifts of Les Deux-Alpes, but far off the snowy mountains of Les Grandes Rousses form a shining horizon.

A clear path takes you down to the lake in a little over an hour. Often snow lies in patches across the trail until mid-summer, but these should be safe enough to cross. The timber-built **Refuge de la Muzelle** (2130m: *accommodation, refreshments*) stands on a grass slope at the northern end of the lake, and the continuing path passes it.

Just beyond the hut the way crosses a bluff and skirts a boggy region, then descends steeply into a lower valley where cascades shower down the steep walls. That on the left is part of the drainage system from the lake. Cross a footbridge over a stream from the right, then a second footbridge takes you over the main stream. From here the path follows the left bank of the torrent which, here and there, pours in more lovely cascades over rocky projections. Soon enter woodland on a good path that loses much height before coming at last to a junction at the foot of the slope. A concrete bridge takes you across the stream and into the hamlet of **L'Alleau**, where there's a campsite. Keep ahead past the houses and through a car park to enter **Bourg d'Arud** (942m: *accommodation, refreshments*) in the Vallée du Vénéon.

Bourg also has a campsite, as well as hotel accommodation and gîtes d'étape: L'Oratoire (☎ 04 76 80 26 36), Le Champ du Moulin (☎ 04 76 80 07 38) and La Reboule (☎ 04 76 80 28 93). The village is also on a daily (infrequent) bus route between Bourg d'Oisans and La Bérarde. For further information about Bourg d'Arud and the Vallée du Vénéon, please see the following section.

View on the descent from Col de Côte-Belle to Valsenestre (Route 49)

South of Col de la Muzelle, a cloud sea fills the valley (Route 50)

Lac Lauvitel: one of the gems of the Écrins National Park (Routes 52 & 54)

The Vallonnet, at the head of the lovely Vallon de Lanchâtra (Route 55)

St-Christophe-en Osians, in the Vallée du Vénéon (Routes 56 and 57)

Peaks, glacial remnants and screes in the Vallée de la Selle (Route 56)

First view of the Lavey glen from Le Souchey (Route 57)

VALLÉE DU VÉNÉON

This deep U-shaped valley, which owes its dramatic qualities to the receding glaciers, drains the very heart of the massif and is one of the most enticing of all the Alps. The casual visitor may find it austere, but its many trails help unravel the essential Écrins – a landscape of extremes. Untamed and unquestionably beautiful, remote sanctuaries lie hidden to all but the most determined of walkers under headwalls of its feeder glens.

ACCESS AND INFORMATION

Location: Southeast of Bourg d'Oisans, the valley penetrates into the heart of the Massif des Écrins south of the Romanche and north of the upper reaches of the Valgaudemar

Bases: Venosc (1019m), Bourg d'Arud (942m), St-Christophe-en-Oisans (1470m), La Bérarde (1713m)

Information: Syndicat d'Initiative, Place de la Télécabine, 38520 Venosc (☎ 04 76 80 06 82)

Office du Tourisme, 38520 St-Christophe-en-Oisans (☎ 04 76 80 50 01)

Office du Tourisme, 38143 La Bérarde (☎ 04 76 79 21 17 – summer only)

Access: By D530 road from Bourg d'Oisans, which forks south from the Bourg to Lautaret road at Le Clapier. From St-Christophe to La Bérarde the road is narrow, subject to stonefall in inclement weather, and is sometimes cut by landslips. Caution is required of all driving on it. It is usually closed in winter above St-Christophe. In summer the valley is served by twice-daily bus from Bourg d'Oisans to La Bérarde.

VALLÉE DU VÉ

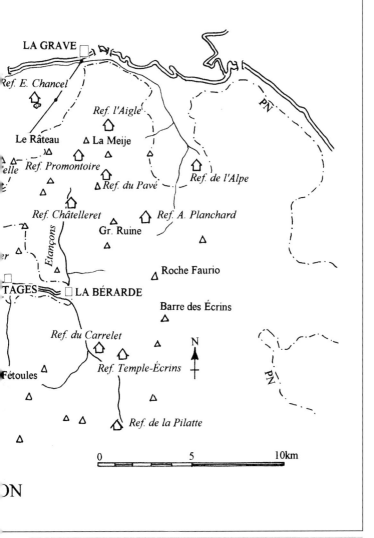

LA GRAVE

Ref. E. Chancel

Le Râteau △ La Meije
△
Ref. l'Aigle

PN

Ref. Promontoire
△ Ref. du Pavé
Ref. de l'Alpe

Ref. Châtelleret
Gr. Ruine
△
Ref. A. Planchard
△

Étançons

Roche Faurio
△

TAGES △ LA BÉRARDE

Barre des Écrins
△

Ref. du Carrelet
△
N

Fétoules △
Ref. Temple-Écrins

△
PN

△
Ref. de la Pilatte

△

0   5   10km

ON

INTRODUCTION

Some of the most exciting mountain scenery and, arguably, the best walking of the Parc National des Écrins is concentrated on the Vallée du Vénéon. With several tributary valleys feeding from north and south, each of which is adorned either by a gleaming lake or two, or headed by a glacial cirque of awesome beauty, the Vénéon's scope is enhanced as a base for a walking holiday. But it should be stressed that there are few gentle walks to be had here. On the contrary most are quite demanding, for the terrain is harsh and uncompromising – especially in the upper valley, the Haut Vénéon, where there are some steep ascents and descents to contend with. Yet rewards are there aplenty.

After branching away from the Vallée de la Romanche at the entrance to the Infernet gorge some 5½km from Bourg d'Oisans, the Vénéon road runs briefly and easily through a flat plain before curving into a narrower valley with wooded lower slopes. As the road curves southeastward, a depression in the southern wall is seen ahead and a minor road breaks away to La Danchère, which huddles below it. La Danchère is just a small village, but from it paths climb into that depression, which opens as a charming hanging valley where the Lac Lauvitel lies – a popular destination for walkers.

The Vénéon road rises a little towards Bourg d'Arud, passing a turning left to Venosc and the valley station of a gondola cableway which serves Les Deux-Alpes, the purpose-built ski resort set upon the ridge that stands between the Vénéon and Vallée de la Romanche. Shortly after this you enter modest Bourg d'Arud, an old stone-walled village built astride the road. Immediately to the east the valley narrows even more, constricted by sharp rock walls, while a cascade seen to the south does little more than provide a hint that above Bourg d'Arud lies another hanging valley with its own tarn, Lac de la Muzelle.

Leaving Bourg the D530 crosses to the south bank of the river and, snaking through the narrows, emerges to a wilder, rockier and less-wooded valley section with a view ahead to the graceful Tête des Fétoules. At Pont du Lac the road recrosses to the Vénéon's true right bank – now the east side – where the valley is at its widest. Off to the right (southwest) a waterfall bursts from a defile which hides the Vallon de Lanchâtra. Tucked in that defile, and unseen from the road, is the little hamlet of Lanchâtra. Beyond it the glen is uninhabited apart from a lone shepherd's hut midway through the valley, but its scant upper pastures lie in a glorious wild cirque well worth the effort spent reaching it.

At Plan du Lac the road begins the steeply twisting climb to St-Christophe-en-Oisans. Although only a small, one-street village which squeezes the road, St-Christophe is the main centre for the Haut Vénéon whose *commune* (or parish), though said to be one of the largest in France, has barely 30 occupants in winter. The village has long been noted for its mountain guides, and was the birthplace of Pierre Gaspard, who guided the first ascent of La Meije in 1877. His memorial is found beside the church. Behind the village lies the Vallée de la Selle, which digs eastward into the high mountains, with Le Râteau at its head and the Massif du Soreiller forming its southern wall.

Out of St-Christophe the road runs along the steep wall of the valley high above the river passing only the tiniest of hamlets, while on the far side of the Vénéon two more tributary valleys cleave the mountains. The first of these is the Mariande glen, the second the Vallon de la Lavey, with a booming cascade at its outflow and a comfortable refuge set among pastures below the Aiguille de l'Olan near its head – a real gem of a valley accessible from the few buildings of Champorent.

It is at Champorent that the valley curves to the northeast, the road (closed from November to May) passing through a few short tunnels and hugging the cliffs while the hillside plunges steeply to the river. But the way eases again as it approaches the hamlet of Les Etages, another huddle of buildings giving access to the very steep and ravine-like Soreiller glen to the north, and the Vallon des Etages to the south. From here to La Bérarde the bed of the valley is partly wooded, but the walling mountains remain austere, rocky and uncompromisingly severe.

La Bérarde is the final settlement at the roadhead. A major mountaineering centre, it sits at the confluence of the upper Vénéon and Etançons valleys, with several refuges nearby which inspire walks to dramatic locations among some of the district's highest mountains.

MAIN VALLEY BASES

- **VENOSC** (1019m) is an attractive, if somewhat twee, village perched above the valley and reached by a twisting road a short distance west of Bourg d'Arud. The narrow streets and alleyways are paved; there's a large car park and gondola lift to Les Deux-Alpes. The tourist office is situated below the village, beside the main D530 road, where there's national park information available. Venosc has several small shops, bars and a restaurant, and accommodation is to be found in the hotel Les Amis de la Montagne (☎ 04 76 80 06 94), which arranges guided walks for guests. There's also a Gîte de France, Le Courtil (☎ 04 76 80 07 41).

- **BOURG D'ARUD** (942m) has two campsites: one just west of the village, the other to the south across the river in the neighbouring hamlet of L'Alleau. There are no shops in Bourg d'Arud, although the campsite Le Champ du Moulin, west of the village, has a small on-site foodstore, bar and restaurant, as well as a *gîte d'étape* (☎ 04 76 80 07 38). Bourg has other *gîte* accommodation at L'Oratoire (☎ 04 76 80 26 36) and La Reboule (☎ 04 76 80 28 93), and the following hotels: Le Grand Rochail (☎ 04 76 80 07 77) and the 17th-century Le Chateau de la Muzelle (☎ 04 76 80 06 71).

- **ST-CHRISTOPHE-EN-OISANS** (1470m) enjoys very fine views of glacier mountains from its location high above the riverbed. The tourist office is found beside the road just below the village, while accommodation is to be had in two hotels, La Table du Chritolet (5 rooms, open mid-April to mid-Nov: ☎ 04 76 69 55 72) and La Cordée, which also has a simple *gîte* attached (9 rooms, 25 dorm places: open all year: ☎ 04 76 79 52 37) and a unique mountain ambience.

- **LA BÉRARDE** (1713m) at the roadhead is crowded with climbers and walkers during the short summer season when accommodation is at a premium. The municipal campsite (open June to end Sept: ☎ 04 76 79 20 45), on the south bank of the river immediately before you enter the village, is, however, large enough for 165 tents. La Bérarde has limited hotel accommodation at Hotel Tairraz (12 rooms and 10 dorm places, open May–Sept: ☎ 04 76 79 53 46), and *chambres d'hôte / gîte de séjour* in Le Champ de Pin (4 rooms and 14 dorm places, open April–Oct: ☎ 04 76 79 54 09). The Creperie l'Atre has 30 dormitory places (☎ 04 76 79 21 55), while the CAF has a large Centre Alpin Français in the village with 172 places in dorms and rooms (manned April–Sept: ☎ 04 76 79 53 83), while the Centre Alpin Belge 'Le Chamois' has 40 places (☎ 04 76 79 05 64). In La Bérarde there are bar/restaurants, a foodstore, tourist office and Bureau des Guides (☎ 04 76 79 54 83).

OTHER VALLEY BASES

Useful for walkers planning to visit Lac Lauvitel, **LA DANCHÈRE** (989m) has hotel facilities in the Auberge du Lac.

In the upper valley, the Haut Vénéon, several hamlets offer accommodation worth considering. At **PLAN DU LAC** (1178m), just below the hairpins which take the road up to St-Christophe, there's a campsite, Les Fetoules (open June to mid-Sept: ☎ 04 76 80 23 99) and a *gîte d'étape*, Gîte du Plan du Lac (rooms and dorms, open all year: ☎ 04 76 80 19 19), while the hamlet of **PRÉ CLOT** (1580m), a short distance upvalley from St-Christophe, has the Gîte les Arias with 10 dormitory places, 4 bedrooms, a bar and restaurant (open all year: ☎ 04 76 79 27 41). Finally, about 3½km before reaching La Bérarde, the small hamlet of **LES ETAGES** (1597m) has the Hôtel du Vallon (☎ 04 76 79 52 18) and Hôtel les Alpinistes (☎ 04 76 79 54 58), both with 8 rooms and open from May to October.

MOUNTAIN HUTS

A number of refuges are accessible to walkers in the Vallée du Vénéon and its tributary valleys, and routes are given below. Remember that reservations are essential for overnight stays.

- **REFUGE DE LA MUZELLE** (2130m) is owned by the Venosc *commune*. Overlooking the lake of the same name, about

4–4½hrs from Bourg d'Arud via GR54, this chalet-style timber-built refuge has 52 places (9 in winter) and a guardian in residence from end of June to end of September, when meals are provided (☎ 04 76 79 02 01).

- **REFUGE DE L'ALPE DU PIN** (1820m) is a fully-equipped but unmanned hut with 30 places set on the south side of the Vénéon and reached by a walk of a little under 2hrs from St-Christophe. It is owned by the JDA (Jarrets d'Acier of Grenoble). (For reservations contact Hôtel La Cordée in St-Christophe: ☎ 04 76 79 52 37.)

- **REFUGE DE LA SELLE** (2673m) overlooks the head of the Vallon de la Selle northeast of St-Christophe, by which it is reached in about 3½hrs. The original hut has been enlarged and modernised, with a fanciful extension that projects over a rock wall. With 80 spaces (16 in winter) it has a guardian from mid-June to mid-Sept and meals provision (☎ 04 76 79 56 56). The hut is owned by the Societé des Touristes du Dauphiné (STD).

- **REFUGE SOREILLER** (2730m) is another STD hut, this one located in a prime position for climbers tackling the pinnacles of the Soreiller massif – most notably the Aiguille Dibona. Reached by a steep walk of around 3hrs from Les Etages, the refuge has 94 places (40 in winter) and a guardian from mid-June to mid-Sept who provides meals (☎ 04 76 79 08 32).

- **REFUGE DE LA LAVEY** (1797m) is owned by the Grenoble section of the CAF. It sits amid pastureland near the head of the Vallon de la Lavey, with Aiguille de l'Olan towering to the south. Reached by a very pleasant walk of 1½hrs from Champorent, or 2¾hrs from St-Christophe, the refuge is manned from mid-June to mid-Sept, and can sleep 72 (30 in winter) in its dormitories (☎ 04 76 80 50 52).

- **REFUGE DU CHATELLERET** (2221m) stands midway up the Etançons valley en route to La Meije, whose South Face looks so impressive on the walk-in; 2¼hrs from La Bérarde. Owned by the CAF it is a large, sturdy-looking building with 90 places (62 in winter) and a resident guardian from mid-June to mid-September, when meals are provided (☎ 04 76 79 08 27).

- **REFUGE DU PROMONTOIRE** (3092m) is included in this list for interest only, as the route to it is beyond the scope of this guide since it crosses crevassed glacier slopes (ice axe, rope, etc, required). Used by climbers tackling routes on La Meije, the refuge is 5hrs from La Bérarde (between the Chatelleret hut and La Meije), is owned by the CAF and has 30 places. The guardian is usually in residence from mid-April to mid-May, and from late June to mid-September (☎ 04 76 80 51 67).

- **REFUGE DU CARRELET** (1908m) is privately owned and easily reached by a valley walk of just 1hr from La Bérarde. The hut stands in the little Plan du Carrelet opposite the Vallon du Chardon, southeast of La Bérarde. It can sleep 50 (15 in winter) and is manned from mid-June to mid-September and at certain weekends either side of those dates. Restaurant service (☎ 04 76 79 25 38).

- **REFUGE DU TEMPLE ÉCRINS** (2410m) is a low, flat-roofed, barrack-like building in a spectacular position under a glacial cirque headed by the Barre des Écrins and Pic Coolidge. The path to it breaks out of the upper Vénéon's valley a short distance upstream of the Carrelet hut, and is gained about 2½hrs from La Bérarde. With 100 places (50 in winter), there's a guardian between mid-June and mid-Sept, when meals are available (☎ 04 76 79 08 28). CAF-owned.

- **REFUGE DE LA PILATTE** (2572m) looks directly onto the Pilatte Glacier, which cascades down the face of Les Bans at the head of the Vallée du Vénéon, about 3–3½hrs from La Bérarde. It's a large, well-equipped building, owned by the Grenoble section of the CAF and with places for 120 (28 in winter). The guardian is usually resident, with meals provision, in the spring (mid-April to mid-May), then weekends, and constantly from mid-June to mid-September (☎ 04 76 79 08 26).

Route 51: Bourg d'Arud (942m) – La Danchère (989m)

Grade:	1
Distance:	4½ kilometres (one way)
Height gain:	47 metres
Time:	1½hrs
Location:	West of Bourg d'Arud

A pleasant woodland and part-riverside walk links Bourg d'Arud with the hamlet of La Danchère, the latter being situated below the famed Lac Lauvitel, which makes an obvious extension to the walk (see Route 52), although on its own the route described here makes a good excuse for an easy morning (or afternoon) stroll, with refreshments on offer once you reach La Danchère.

From Bourg d'Arud cross the road bridge over the Vénéon and bear right through a parking area into the hamlet of L'Alleau. Wander up the path between houses (GR54 waymarks) and cross a footbridge over a stream. Turn right on the crossing path (the left-hand option goes to Refuge de la Muzelle). This well-made trail enters woodland and remains within it nearly all the way to La Danchère. There are several alternative paths cutting from it, but the main route should be obvious with occasional red-white waymarks.

On coming to a major fork, where the right-hand track slopes downhill, take the left branch rising in the woods. The path is an undulating one, twisting among trees. At first it takes you high above the Vénéon, then descends to river level – all very attractive, especially alongside the river.

After about 30mins come to a concrete footbridge spanning the Vénéon. Do not cross but continue ahead on the left bank (a sign here gives 1hr to La Danchère). Shortly after this you cross a rock- and mud-chute, then resume beside the river. After keeping company with the Vénéon for some time, the path works away from it, rising to cross an avalanche runnel.

After about 1hr 15mins come to a major crossing path. (The right-hand branch slopes downhill to Les Escallons and Les Gauchoirs.) Ignoring this option turn left and rise to join a road, walk ahead and within a few minutes you will arrive in **La Danchère** (989m: *accommodation, refreshments*). Even if you do not intend to visit Lac Lauvitel, do continue a short way beyond the Auberge du Lac to visit the old buildings that comprise the hamlet. Practically the last building on the path to Lac Lauvitel is a *buvette* providing refreshments.

Return to Bourg d'Oisans by the same path, allowing about 1hr 15mins.

Route 52: La Danchère (989m) – Lac Lauvitel (1540m)

Grade:	2
Distance:	3 kilometres (one way)
Height gain:	551 metres
Time:	1½hrs
Location:	Southwest of Bourg d'Arud

Lac Lauvitel is attractively set in a deep mountain bowl to the south of La Danchère, and the walk to it is one of the most popular in the national park. The approach leads through mixed woods, and climbs beside streams and cascades before coming to more open but vegetated country with wild raspberries, bilberries and juniper carpeting the hillside above the lake. There being no refreshment facilities at the lake, and it making a perfect site for a picnic, do not forget to take food and drink with you. Should you have your own transport, there's plenty of parking space in La Danchère.

From the top end of La Danchère the metalled road gives way to a rough track. This leads to a stream and forks. Both options lead to the lake in 1½hrs – the left-hand path goes by La Selles, the right-hand trail via La Rousse. The suggestion here is to ascend by way of the La Rousse path and descend via La Selles.

Cross the stream (immediately over this a *variante* of GR54 cuts right to Les Gouchoirs and Bourg d'Oisans) and ascend a stony path that rises among shrubs then woodland, with minor streams here and there. Another path junction is met below a series of cascades, and we continue on the right-hand option, now entering the Parc National des Écrins. This part of the walk becomes more open, although there's still some woodland cover, but eventually you top a rise near a small stone building. Pass this to your left and come to a water supply, just beyond which the path forks again. Below and ahead lies **Lac Lauvitel**; the east and west sides of the valley rise steeply, while at the southern end an alluvial fan adorned with trees is backed by a seductive glen. A little way ahead across a sloping meadow you gain a fine 'ring-circle' view which is rather more secluded than the open meadows at the northeast corner of the lake.

There are **three options** from here:

- take the right-hand path at the trail junction, to climb to Lac du Plan Vianney (2hrs) and Brêche du Périer (2½hrs) on a GR54 *variante*;
- bear left across a rocky section among wild raspberries to gain the lake's northeast corner then follow a faint path round and above the eastern shore towards the southern end (during research this path had been cut by rockfall at a ledge crossing a cliff shortly before the far end could be reached) – allow 30–45mins;
- take the path which rises from the northeast corner of the lake in zigzags to Col du Vallon (2½hrs) and Refuge de la Muzelle (3½hrs) – this is described in reverse as Route 54 below.

Return to La Danchère in 45mins by way of a good path from the lake's northeast corner.

Route 53: Bourg d'Arud (942m) – Refuge de la Muzelle (2130m)

Grade:	3
Distance:	6 kilometres (one way)
Height gain:	1188 metres
Time:	4hrs (2½hrs down)
Location:	SSW of Bourg d'Arud

Owned by the commune of Venosc the chalet-style Refuge de la Muzelle is superbly situated in pastoral country overlooking the lake of the same name, with the 3465m Roche de la Muzelle and its glacier reflected in the water. The refuge is visited by trekkers on the Tour de l'Oisans (see Route 50), usually approached from the opposite direction to the present walk. It's a steep path which climbs from L'Alleau through woods and alongside a series of cascades before coming to the head of a cirque, where more waterfalls are seen at close quarters. From here the way zigzags steeply to gain the basin in which the hut is set. Though quite demanding, it's a fine walk with lots of interest, while the hut itself makes an atmospheric night's lodging.

Beginning in the centre of Bourg d'Arud, cross the road bridge over the Vénéon and turn right into L'Alleau. Walk through the hamlet and cross a footbridge over the Pisse torrent (which begins at Lac de la Muzelle). Turn left on a major crossing path – a partially-paved old mule path which rises into woodland. On coming to the national park boundary a seat beside the trail gives a good view across the valley to Venosc, and about 2mins later you pass the remains of a simple shelter dug into the steep hillside.

At first the path was remorseless with zigzags, but it now eases into a pleasant leftward slant with the sound of a waterfall crashing not far off. At a junction of paths (Le Cerisier), where there's another seat and a water supply, ignore the left-hand trail (to Laffreyte, 30mins) and continue ahead on the main path. Soon rise on the right-hand side of the torrent – ahead a waterfall is seen bursting over rocks – and the path resumes its zigzag ascent, brings you to a close view of another waterfall, then goes alongside a succession of cascades, leaving woodland behind.

Following the torrent all the way, the trail goes through a narrow ravine, at the head of which there's a tightly-enclosed cirque with more waterfalls spraying from the south headwall and from the eastern slopes. Cross the stream on a footbridge (1798m, 3hrs 15mins), where a sign gives 45mins to the lake. The way now takes you below the east side waterfall, then zigzags up the slope beyond where views become severely restricted. Climbing through a narrow V-wedge, then steeply up the right flank, the path then eases to skirt a marshy basin before passing through a grassy saddle to find Lac de la Muzell lying below, the flat-roofed **Refuge de la Muzelle** (2130m: *accommodation, refreshments*) just above it, and a farm building nearby.

Options from here include:

- ascent of the 2400m Roche Percée (1½hrs), which is a superb viewpoint;
- approach to the Glacier de la Muzelle;
- a 2hr uphill walk to the Cime du Pied de Barry (2500m) on the ridge east of the hut;
- a steep walk up to Col de la Muzelle (2625m, 1½hrs);
- a crossing of Col du Vallon (1½hrs) to Lac Lauvitel (3½hrs) as described in Route 54 below.

Allow 2½hrs for the descent to Bourg d'Arud by the same path.

Route 54: Refuge de la Muzelle (2130m) – Col du Vallon (2531m) – Lac Lauvitel (1540m) – Bourg d'Arud (942m)

Grade:	3
Distance:	13 kilometres
Height gain:	401 metres
Height loss:	1589 metres
Time:	5½–6hrs
Location:	Southwest of Bourg d'Arud

By combining this with Route 53 a super circuit can be achieved – a classic of the region. Col du Vallon is the link, a pass in a ridge running north from Tête de la Muraillette, west of Lac de la Muzelle. On the east (Muzelle) side of the col there are no waymarks, although the path is mostly clear. On the descent to Lac Lauvitel, on the other hand, there are numerous waymarks – but these are needed in poor visibility, for the way crosses lots of rocky areas where clear paths will not be found. The col (apparently) enjoys fine views. I cannot confirm this as on my crossing clouds hung from lake to lake and there was nothing to be seen!

Go down to the lake from Refuge de la Muzelle and walk along its right-hand (western) shore. Immediately after crossing the outflow stream, leave the shoreline path and veer right on an alternative trail (there are neither signs nor waymarks for this). Ignoring other minor paths which cut from it, go along the right-hand side of a small pool and curve right to a small sign by a fork. During research this was the only sign on the east side of Col du Vallon. Take the left branch, where the path is directed into a rock tip to be guided by cairns rising across the rocks and boulders. Having gained about 60m of height, the path contours to the right then makes a series of loops which become tight zigzags leading up to another rocky area.

Cross the Combe des Ruines and zigzag towards the col, where the gradient steepens near the top – on the uppermost 70m or so the path is buttressed by long pine branches. So gain **Col du Vallon** about 1¼–1½hrs from the refuge. (A sign on the col gives the altitude as 2540m, while the map says 2531m.)

Here you overlook a rocky basin – apparently in clear conditions the view back shows both the Lac and Refuge de la Muzelle. Bear left and wander along the ridge for about 100m, then follow red-white waymarks down to the right, descending into and across the basin of rocks, boulders and slabs, heading north then veering west as the rough descent continues. (**Note:** although the map does not show it, there appears to be a more obvious path well to the right of the waymarked route, but visibility was insufficient to gain much useful information.) The waymarked route veers north again, until at the bottom of a rocky section you come to rough pastures and a shepherd's hut marked on the map as Cabane de l'Embernard (2116m), which you pass to your right.

Below the *cabane* the trail leads down to a stream, which you cross and continue along its right-hand side on a much better path, which now slants right then twists down again to negotiate the Côte de la Traversette. This involves crossing a sort of col, then cutting sharply to the right on very steep ground to cross a gully, then going up to turn a rocky shoulder, beyond which you're on more open ground again with views down to **Lac Lauvitel**. The way leads down to it with numerous loops and zigzags, reaching the north-eastern end of the lake about 2hrs from Col du Vallon.

Descend the signed path to La Danchère via La Selles. This is an easy descent, partially through woodland, sometimes alongside the outflow stream from the lake, now and then with close views of waterfalls. And it leads without complication to **La Danchère** (989m: *accommodation, refreshments*) in about 45mins. Walk down the road to pass the Auberge du Lac, and shortly after, as the road curves gently to the left, take a signed path descending directly ahead. About 2mins later turn right at a junction and follow this pleasant woodland path all the way to the concrete footbridge at L'Alleau, where the path to Refuge de la Muzelle begins. Bear left across the stream and wander through L'Alleau to **Bourg d'Arud**.

Other Walks from Bourg d'Arud

- On the south side of the valley a circular walk of about 1½hrs via the ruins of **LAFFREYTE** begins by following the GR54 trail taken in Route 53 (to Refuge de la Muzelle) as far as the woodland path junction at Le Cerisier, then turning left to Laffreyte, and descending from there back to L'Alleau and Bourg. Another, on the same side of the Vénéon, climbs to the high point of **CHAMP DE L'AIGUILLE** (1500m) in 2hrs – this path is also reached by the footbridge above L'Alleau.

- **VENOSC** is easily reached in 15mins by a comfortably-angled path which begins behind the hotel Le Grand Rochail and rises mostly through woodland, while above Venosc there's a 500m *via ferrata*, **VIA FERRATA DES PERRONS**, that climbs to 1720m and exits onto a path leading to Les Deux-Alpes.

- A final stage of the Tour de l'Oisans leads to **BOURG D'OISANS** via La Danchère and Les Gauchoirs in about 4hrs, and in the opposite direction (heading southeast) a linking of paths leads to **PONT DU PLAN DU LAC** in 50mins.

Route 55: Pont du Plan du Lac (1171m) – Vallon de Lanchâtra (2260m)

Grade:	3
Distance:	7½ kilometres (one way)
Height gain:	1089 metres
Time:	3½–4hrs (2½hrs return)
Location:	On the south side of the valley between Bourg d'Arud and St-Christophe

Flowing parallel with the Vallon de la Muzelle, the Lanchâtra is a very narrow, V-wedge of a glen that rises quite steeply to the south, its highest reaches kept secret until the very last. And then what a surprise is in store! The Vallonnet, as this upper region is called, is very much a sanctuary, a levelling of pastures unguessed from below, contained within a lovely glacial cirque. The ragged mountains that form this cirque wear small glaciers which add much to the scene. It may take some effort to gain the Vallonnet, but it's well worth it.

The Bourg d'Oisans to La Bérarde bus will stop at Pont du Plan du Lac if requested. For walkers with their own transport there's parking space on the left (river side) of the road, just before it curves to cross the bridge. Alternatively, if you're based in Bourg d'Arud without transport and miss the morning bus, it will take only 50mins to walk to Pont du Plan du Lac by a combination of footpath and road.

From the road at Pont du Plan du Lac a signed path cuts southeast as the road bends left, leading through a grove of birch trees and alongside the milky-blue Vénéon river. The snowy Tête des Fetoules stands magnificently upvalley. Leaving the riverside, the path begins to gain height gradually, and in about 25mins you come to a junction. (The left-hand trail leads to the *gîte* and campsite at Plan du Lac.) Continue ahead, now zigzagging steeply to gain entry to the **Vallon de Lanchâtra**, which is guarded by a very narrow gorge out of which explodes the Cascade de la Pisse. The climb is mostly in the shade of trees, and about 1hr from the road you enter the little hamlet of Lanchâtra (1430m), which consists of a few occupied houses, several ruined buildings and a chapel. (About 5mins beyond the hamlet you pass a ruined watermill, whose millstone can be seen from the path.)

Lanchâtra is idyllically situated at the entrance to the valley, but with views out to the Vénéon. The path twists through the hamlet and descends to a water supply. (An alternative path breaks off to the right, marked 'Crêtes', which offers a way of crossing to the Refuge de la Muzelle.) Our path continues through woodland and soon comes to another junction, where the left-hand option is a descent route to Plan du Lac via the east side of the gorge. Remain on the right-hand side of the river and continue ahead, rising easily to a brief level area where the river is more placid than hitherto. The way then goes through a little grove of trees and swings left to cross a footbridge over the Ruisseau de la Pisse at 1575m. A sign here gives 45mins to 'Cabane Pastorale' and 2hrs to 'Glacier'.

Now the valley curves to the south, and the path climbs again. Across the valley at this bend a large area of hillside reveals an expanse of dark-grey shale, by contrast with the rest of the valley wall which is mostly grass-covered. The way continues to rise through the valley, then with a burst of zigzags it passes to the right of the shepherd's hut (the 'Cabane Pastorale') and maintains direction upvalley to gain another grassy bluff.

Beyond this the trail strikes across the hillside, then makes some long loops from which you catch views north to the distant snowy Grandes Rousses, while the head of the Lanchâtra glen begins to reveal its glaciers. Gaining more height now in zigzags you come to a brief band of rocks, where the path has one or two delicate (but not difficult) scrambly manouvres to make before contouring southwest, with the Vallonnet slowly revealing itself ahead and below. Views now are tremendous, and at the end of the contouring section the trail slopes down to these upper pastures, crossing a few short rock slabs on the way.

The Vallonnet surely is a 'sanctuary', for its beauty could not be guessed from below. The main stream is fed by others coming from right and left, while the small glaciers that hang from mountains rimming the cirque drain first into screes. The whole area is utterly charming. Simply wander as far as you choose, or collapse beside the stream and allow the hours to drift. But allow at least 2½hrs for the return to Pont du Plan du Lac by the same path.

Other Walks from Plan du Lac

- On the east side of the Vénéon, shortly after the road crosses at Pont du Plan du Lac, a path cuts up the hillside then strikes south-east in a pleasant traverse to the traditional Oisans hamlet of **LE PUY** (1583m) in about 45mins. This path continues to **ST-CHRISTOPHE**, or the walk could be varied (and extended in challenge) by rising from Le Puy to the viewpoint of the **TÊTE DE LA TOURA** (2885m), which guards the entrance to the Vallée de la Selle.
- Also from Plan du Lac, and starting near Camping des

Fétoules, there's a two-stage *via ferrata* which climbs the mountainside towards St-Christophe and passes west of the village on the second stage. The **VIA FERRATA DE ST-CHRISTOPHE** takes around 3½hrs to complete. Information about this route can be gathered at the Plan du Lac *gîte* which is open all year.

Route 56: St-Christophe-en-Oisans (1470m) – Refuge de la Selle (2673m)

Grade:	2–3
Distance:	8 kilometres (one way)
Height gain:	1203 metres
Time:	3½-4hrs (2½hrs down)
Location:	Northeast of St-Christophe

The Vallée de la Selle is a long, narrow, but attractive glen whose southern wall is dominated by the North Face of the Aiguille du Plat de la Selle and the big walls of the Massif du Soreiller, while Le Râteau (near neighbour of La Meije) heads the valley above the Glacier de la Selle. For most of the walk these peaks will hold your attention. They seduce from afar and do not disappoint on closer acquaintance. As for the refuge, it is an astonishingly modernistic piece of architecture; from below it looks like a cross between a snow-mobile and some imaginative space probe. Definitely not in the traditional mould! But it is comfortable and welcoming.

There are two possible beginnings to this walk. One is signed between buildings on the north side of the road in the centre of St-Christophe. The other is found just north of the church, and it is this that is described here. (The first-mentioned route soon joins it.)

On the down-valley side of the church a minor road goes up a slope towards a house just a few paces above the main road. A sign here indicates the start of walks to Ref. de la Selle, Les Pres, Miroir des Fétoules, Le Puy and Leyrette. When this minor road ends a footpath leads between houses, and 3mins from the start it forks. Bear right and climb steeply among trees, so to reach a road at the few buildings of Leyrette. Cross the road and continue between the buildings, rising up the hillside to the road again. Painted arrows ensure you follow the correct path to avoid the road's hairpins, and finally you regain the road just before it ends (about 20mins from St-Christophe). Walkers with their own transport will find parking spaces here.

Do not take the track which cuts to the right, although it is signed to La Selle, but take the footpath that continues from the roadhead. This crosses the Torrent du Diable, and about 10mins from the roadhead it forks. Continue ahead (the right branch) along the hillside where the valley is narrow and steeply walled, soon passing above a barrage, beyond which the valley has been almost blocked by a rock- and boulder-slide. The path works over this, while ahead the valley curves to the right to give a first view of the pyramid-shaped Le Râteau at its head. Although narrow, the valley is rather more open here than at its entrance, and as you progress through it there are various side streams to cross which come from a succession of waterfalls spraying down the left-hand wall.

For some time the trail is generous, making height easily and with no real demands. At around 2200m it crosses a band of scree and rises to a new level overlooking a flattish gravel plain, which looks as though it could once have been the bed of a small lake. Beyond this to the east the valley rises like a ramp – the terminal moraine of glaciers that have receded far into the mountains. The left-hand slope above the 'gravel pan' is a very flowery one, but this is exchanged for the rocks of the 'ramp', where the path twists more steeply than before. About a third of the way up the slope you're led close to the glacial torrent for a while, and just above this it may be possible to see the curious shape of the refuge overhanging crags high above and to the left.

Eventually come to the upper glacial basin, which is a desert of rocks and boulders. The trail now veers left to climb in loops below the hut, then slants up the final slope to gain the **Refuge de la Selle** (2673m: *accommodation, refreshments*). There are, in fact, two buildings – the original hut (built in traditional style) and the main building with its futuristic, shining metal dining room projecting out from its supporting crags. Views are tremendous, with very impressive rock and raw high mountain scenery in practically every direction.

Route 57: St-Christophe-en-Oisans (1470m) – Refuge de la Lavey (1797m)

Grade:	3
Distance:	17 kilometres (round trip)
Height gain/loss:	1134 metres
Time:	5½hrs
Location:	Southeast of St-Christophe

The Vallon de la Lavey (otherwise known as the Vallée de Muande) is one of the loveliest in the Écrins National Park, and this walk explores both flanks on the way to and from the refuge, which stands idyllically among pastures below the Aiguille de l'Olan. The standard way to approach this hut is from Champorent, some 3km upvalley from St-Christophe where there are parking facilities (see Route 58), but the following route is described for walkers without their own transport.

In the centre of St-Christophe, almost opposite Hotel La Cordée, a path descends below the side of a building on which there's a sign to La Bernardière, Les Granges, Le Clot d'en Bas and Alpe du Pin. The path slopes down below the village and passes the *mairie*, where it forks. The right-hand path goes to the Pont du Diable, but we take the left branch through woodland and onto a minor road. Walk ahead along this, and when it divides continue ahead on the upper branch, and a little over 10mins from the start you pass below the hamlet of La Bernardière. The road forks a second time and you take the lower option, which leads to the few buildings of Le Clot (30mins). The road ends and a footpath continues into forest. When this forks ignore the upper route (which goes to Champorent) and continue ahead, soon twisting down into the Vénéon's gorge, and cross on a footbridge at about 1350m (40mins).

Still in forest the path now climbs to a major junction where you turn left, direction La Bérarde. The way then undulates between trees and forks once more. Take the upper branch signed to Le Souchey and La Lavey (the lower option is the path to La Bérarde). About 1hr 10mins from St-Christophe you come onto a promontory giving a very fine view over the Vénéon, and about 15mins later come to the handful of buildings that comprise Le Souchey at the Lavey valley's entrance.

The medieval stone bridge below Champorent, which gives access to the Vallon de la Lavey (Routes 57, 58)

Beyond Le Souchey the narrow path leaves the forest and pushes along the west flank of the Vallon de la Lavey among wild raspberries and with some splendid views to glacier-hung peaks ahead, waterfalls spraying the hillsides, and the Muande torrent thundering below. After crossing a scree slope the way descends to river level, and about 2hrs 15mins from the start comes to another path junction by a pretty stone-built hump-backed bridge (1701m), which will be crossed later on the walk out.

Continue ahead on the west bank, passing a notable waterfall off to the left then other cascades on the right streaking the hillside. A shepherd's hut (Le Cloutet) is seen on the opposite bank, and shortly after passing this the trail rises easily over a bluff, just beyond which you come to **Refuge de la Lavey** (1797m: *accomodation, refreshments*). Set in lovely pastures, the hut enjoys views to Les Rouies and its glacier at the head of the valley, and to the Aiguille de l'Olan that rises immediately to the south.

Note: Walks to be tackled from the refuge are listed below, and described under Route 59.

For the return to St-Christophe take the same path as that used on the approach, but only as far as the trail junction near the hump-backed bridge (30mins from the hut). Bear right to cross the bridge and wander down the right-hand side of the river. At first over grass, then more rocky, the path leads to the valley entrance, where you gain a fine view down the Vallée du Vénéon and across to Champorent. Over a grassy shoulder the way descends through La Raja – a few stone buildings and a shrine beside the trail. Below this you pass beneath a steep crag and twist down to the confluence of the Muande and Vénéon rivers – the Muande bursting from the narrow gorge in a spectacular waterfall.

At a path junction veer left to skirt a meadow where a two-span wooden bridge crosses the Muande on the left, and a charming hump-backed bridge arches over the Vénéon. For Champorent cross the stone bridge and ascend the slope ahead, but for St-Christophe cross the Muande by the wooden bridge and enter forest. The path eases alongside the river, then climbs steeply before making a belvedere and coming to a junction. It is here that you join the outward route and follow the familiar path back to St-Christophe.

Other Walks from St-Christophe
- Apart from the short, 'local' walks easily accessible from the village, one of the most popular day walks from St-Christophe leads across the valley to the unmanned **REFUGE DE L'ALPE DU PIN** (1820m). It takes only about 2hrs to reach from the village – the way is well signed and it begins almost opposite Hotel Le Cordée – but you'd want to spend some time there before turning back. Alternatively, one could extend the walk from the refuge on a path heading southeast to enter the Vallon de la Mariande, or descend to La Gassaudière before dropping to the river. A visit to the **VALLON DE LA MARIANDE** could also be made from St-Christophe in about 3hrs – this is the short glen which parallels the Vallon de la Lavey to the west, with the Glacier de la Mariande hanging at its head and a tarn, Lac de la Mariande, tucked high on its southwest slope at 2604m.

- A 3hr circular walk could also be made by heading southeast on a path above the road, passing the ruins of Cuculet to reach **PRÉ CLOT**, and continuing from there to the hamlets of **CHAMPÉBRAN** and **CHAMPORENT**, where you then descend through woods above the Vénéon heading northwest to **LE CLOT**, after which you take a minor road to **LA BERNARDIÈRE** and finally up a woodland path back to **ST-CHRISTOPHE**.

Route 58: Champorent Parking (1560m) – Refuge de la Lavey (1797m)

Grade:	2
Distance:	8 kilometres (round trip)
Height gain/loss:	1254 metres
Time:	4hrs
Location:	Southeast of St-Christophe

This is the standard approach route to the Refuge de la Lavey used by walkers with their own transport. The hamlet of Champorent lies about 3km upvalley from St-Christophe, and the parking area is signed.

From the parking area the path is obvious. It descends steeply to the Vénéon river and crosses on a classical arched stone bridge near the river's confluence with the Muande. Do not cross the Muande, which bursts from its gorge in a booming waterfall (there's a two-span wooden bridge), but ascend the slope to its left, ignoring the path which branches left to La Bérarde. The way climbs steeply to the few buildings of La Raja, continues to rise over a bluff and then forges ahead into the Vallon de la Lavey on the east bank of the Muande torrent. The way is uncomplicated, and it eventually brings you to another (but much smaller) hump-backed bridge, which you cross and in a few paces come to a path junction. Bear left, and rising over a grassy knoll you come to the **Refuge de la Lavey** (1797m: *accommodation, refreshments*) about 2¼hrs from the start. See below for walks from the hut, but for the return to Champorent simply reverse the upward route. This will take about 1¾hrs.

Route 59: Refuge de la Lavey (1797m) – Lac des Beches (2401m)

Grade:	2-3
Distance:	2½ kilometres (one way)
Height gain:	620 metres
Time:	1¾–2hrs (1hr return)
Location:	Southwest of the refuge

High above the refuge, in a little rocky cirque under the Aiguilles des Arias, and undetected from below, lies the small glacial tarn known as the Lac des Beches. The way to it is steep, but views from the path and from the lake itself make the effort worthwhile.

Walk upvalley from the refuge, keeping on the right-hand side of the stream, and in 5mins the path forks. That to the Brêche de l'Olan (3hrs via a glacier crossing) continues ahead, but the way to the tarn veers half-right and soon attacks the slope in zigzags through a steep glen backed by the Aiguille de l'Olan. The path then

Refuge de la Lavey (Routes 57–59)

cuts to the right, slanting uphill to reach a grassy shoulder from which you gain a bird's-eye view down onto the refuge.

The trail does not cross the shoulder, but bears left to rise along it before climbing in more zigzags, sometimes quite steeply, to top a rocky crest by which to enter the cirque formed by the Aiguilles des Arias. The milky tarn lies just below. On one side glacier-smoothed slabs dip into the water, on the other a stream flows from it, with views out to the northeast where the Massif du Soreiller – with the Aiguille Dibona prominent – makes a jagged horizon. The way back to the refuge by necessity uses the same path.

Other Walks from Refuge de la Lavey

From the hut it is obvious that one could spend several days here exploring the valley and walling hillsides. As well as Lac des Beches, there are other lakes to visit.

* **LAC DES ROUIES** (2722m) makes a full day's outing (6½hrs in all). This tarn lies southeast of the refuge and is approached from the upper valley, while the tiny **LAC DES FÉTOULES** (2249m) lies at the western foot of the Tête des Fétoules, is reached in 2hrs from the hut, but is not shown on the map.

* Wandering the upper valley as far as the **GLACIER DU FOND** will also make an interesting day out, while experienced mountain trekkers with the necessary equipment to deal with crevassed glaciers have a wealth of opportunities for crossing the high ridge systems that wall the valley.

Route 60: Champorent (1560m) – Les Etages (1597m)

Grade:	1
Distance:	**5 kilometres (one way)**
Height gain:	**217 metres**
Height loss:	**180 metres**
Time:	**1½hrs**
Location:	**Southeast of St-Christophe**

This easy riverside walk is a way of linking the two hamlets which line the road between St-Christophe and La Bérarde. Champorent lies 3km upvalley from St-Christophe and is served by the twice-daily bus to La Bérarde. There's also a pleasant path which runs from St-Christophe to Champorent just above the road (about 1–1½hrs).

Leaving Champorent descend by a well-trodden path to the river (the same path which is used for the route to Refuge de la Lavey), and cross on the lovely hump-backed bridge. The Muande torrent thunders just ahead to the right as it explodes from its gorge. Walk ahead across a meadow, then veer left, and when the path forks moments later take the left branch (direction La Bérarde). This follows the Vénéon upstream along its south bank all the way to Les Etages. Just before reaching the stream which flows from the Vallon des Etages, where there's a disused watermill, cross a bridge over the Vénéon and walk up a service road into the hamlet of **Les Etages** (1597m: *accommodation, refreshments*). To extend the walk as far as La Bérarde, see Route 63.

Route 61: Les Etages (1597m) – Refuge du Soreiller (2730m)

Grade:	3
Distance:	4½ kilometres (one way)
Height gain:	1133 metres
Time:	3–3½hrs (2¼hrs down)
Location:	NNW of Les Etages

The walk up to this hut is through steep and wild country, emerging from a narrow gorge to the Balme basin, above which the Aiguille Dibona (3131m) (see Appendix B) appears like an unscalable needle of rock. At the base of this 400m needle stands Refuge du Soreiller, a large hut owned by the STD, and one that is understandably popular with climbers. It's quite a demanding walk, but an ever-interesting one.

At the western end of Les Etages a prominent sign indicates the start of the path which cuts up the north side of the road. A similar path begins from a grassy area next to the Hôtel les Alpinistes, and the two unite soon after. The way rises in zigzags up the steep rock-strewn hillside, then veers left towards the entrance to the Amont gorge, which is guarded by solemn rock bastions.

It's an extremely narrow gorge with the path twisting up to and into it, and at an altitude of about 1992m a footbridge carries the way across the torrent to its left-hand side. Now climbing in more zigzags, the Aiguille Dibona is seen high above. Near the head of the gorge the path breaks off to the right, and then returns left once more before emerging to an upper basin, the Combe de la Balme. For a short distance the angle eases, then the path rises again in yet more zigzags over increasingly rocky terrain, and comes at last to the **Refuge du Soreiller** (2730m: *accommodation, refreshments*) at the very base of the *aiguille*, on which climbers will frequently be seen working out an assortment of routes.

Route 62: Les Etages (1597m) – Vallon des Etages (2040m)

Grade:	2
Distance:	3 kilometres (one way)
Height gain:	470 metres
Time:	1½hrs
Location:	South of Les Etages

From Les Etages one has only a brief hint of the nature of the glen seen to the south. But walkers who have been to the Soreiller refuge will no doubt have had their interest sparked by long views across the Vénéon, where the Vallon des Etages suggests a wild but attractive hanging valley headed by the glaciated Pointe du Vallon des Etages (3564m) and guarded from the west by the Tête des Fétoules. The glacier that rims the upper part of the glen sweeps down to the north, where it disappears among moraines and streams. This walk explores the lower part of the glen, climbing at first through pinewoods then into the open grass and scree of the valley proper.

Go down the service road below Les Etages, cross the Vénéon by the footbridge, and take the signed path which goes ahead and soon rises through woods on the right-hand side of the torrent, which escapes the *vallon* in a fine waterfall. On leaving the cover of trees you look upstream to where the Pointe and Glacier du Vallon des Etages make an impressive backdrop. Rising steadily towards them the valley becomes increasingly wild and untamed. Eventually the path comes to the terminal moraine of the fast-receding Glacier du Vallon des Etages and crosses to the east side of the stream (1¼–1½hrs). Return downvalley on its right bank – this will take about 45mins, with views of an entirely different order to appreciate on the way.

Route 63: Les Etages (1597m) – *La Bérarde (1713m)*

Grade:	1
Distance:	3½ kilometres
Height gain:	116 metres
Time:	1hr
Location:	East of Les Etages

This is the final leg of an unbroken series of footpaths leading upvalley from Plan du Lac (sections of which appear in Routes 55 and 60), an easy but not uninteresting walk that remains on the south bank of the Vénéon as far as La Bérarde.

From the centre of Les Etages a sign at the roadside indicates the start of the walk, directing the way between buildings, then right onto a short service road and almost immediately left to cross the Vénéon by bridge. Turn left again, and shortly after cross the stream coming from the Vallon des Etages by a disused mill. The path forks and you take the left branch heading upstream. It's a narrow but clear path, and for much of the way it remains among trees, but towards La Bérarde it rises to cross an open rock slide (avalanche area), and soon after reaches the large municipal campsite on the outskirts of the village. Walk through this and either cross the footbridge over the river at the eastern end of the site, or continue on a narrow path which leaves the upper end just beyond a washroom block, then descends to a second footbridge leading to the car park in **La Bérarde** (1713m: *accommodation, refreshments*).

Route 64: La Bérarde (1713m) – Tête de la Maye (2518m)

Grade:	3
Distance:	3 kilometres (one way)
Height gain:	805 metres
Time:	2½hrs
Location:	North of La Bérarde

Overlooking La Bérarde from the north, the Tête de la Maye is surely one of the great Alpine viewpoints – certainly there are few (if any) in the Écrins that can better it, so far as walkers are concerned. But the route is not for the faint-hearted. It is very exposed in numerous places, and has many 'scrambly' sections safeguarded with fixed chains, cables and/or metal rungs. It is not in the same league as a via ferrata, but neither is it a straightforward stroll, although it should not daunt any practised hillwalker. And the summit panorama compensates for the effort required to gain it.

About 40m downstream of the road bridge at the entrance to La Bérarde, a footpath cuts north, signed to Promontoire, Bonne Pierre, Châtelleret and La Maye. Rising steadily into the Etançons glen there are several braidings to this path, but they converge before the Tête de la Maye junction is reached. This comes after about 25mins (1885m) and is signed. Turning left the way now climbs in numerous zigzags, passing through different belts of vegetation, and with views growing in extent as height is gained.

After rising nearly 400m from the road, the trail veers left and, at about 2100m, comes to the first in a series of slabs whose ascent is aided by fixed chain and metal rungs. There are many such pitches between here and a prominent shoulder below the summit, with twisting paths and gritty ledges in between. Please take care not to dislodge stones as rock climbers tackle the longer slabs, above which the path makes an occasional traverse. Eventually come onto a grassy shoulder marked with several cairns and with tremendous views to enjoy, but you skirt this to the right in order to make the final 100m or so of ascent from the Vallée du Vénénon side of the Tête.

The **Tête de la Maye** is a large domed summit of rock and grass, on which there's an orientation table giving names of every mountain in view – and there are many, for there's a 360° panorama of stunning beauty. To the north lies La Meije with the Brêche de la Meije (a notable col between it and Le Râteau, which looks so different to the view from above La Grave). A long ridge system to the northeast has the flat-topped summit of Pic Bourcat rising from it; then comes the deep Vallon de Bonne Pierre to the east, with the finest mountain in all that view, the Dôme de Neige des Écrins. Next, but further away to the southeast, is the impressive rock wall of l'Ailefroide, then the snow and ice of Les Bans to the south-southeast at the very head of the Vénéon, while downvalley a welter of mountains crowds the view, most without snow or ice, but Roche de la Muzelle is an exception with its glacial armoury. Just across and above La Bérarde, the Grande Aiguille de la Bérarde looks fine, while to its left (southeast), with a glacier tongue projecting towards the valley, is the Cime de l'Encoula.

Allow at least 1½hrs for the descent by the same route.

Route 65: La Bérarde (1713m) – Vallon de Bonne Pierre (2944m)

Grade:	2–3
Distance:	5½ kilometres (one way)
Height gain:	1231 metres
Time:	3½hrs (2–2½hrs return)
Location:	Northeast of La Bérarde

Draining westward into the Etançons glen just above La Bérarde, from a tight little cirque rimmed by a jagged skyline of rock peaks, the Vallon de Bonne Pierre is full of wild grandeur. Seen from the summit of Tête de la Maye it is extremely appealing, yet its steepness is misjudged. When viewed from the Etançons glen it is so foreshortened as to have its true identity veiled. So this walk serves as an introduction. Although the high point of the walk is given as 2944m, at the edge of the firn basin below Roche Faurio, it is not necessary to go that far to enjoy the wild aspect of this glen. Simply wander as far as you care to go to feel enclosed by the great peaks. Enjoy their ruggedness, then turn back.

Take the tarmac footpath heading north alongside the Bureau des Guides in the centre of La Bérarde. The tarmac soon ends and the path forks. Take the right branch to rise in gentle windings among trees and shrubs, working a way above the village into the Vallon des Etançons. After about 25mins you enter the national park, and shortly after cross the Bonne Pierre torrent on a footbridge at 1873m. On the north side of the torrent the path forks again.

Bear right, steadily making height into the **Vallon de Bonne Pierre**, keeping the torrent to your right. As the way progresses, so the landscape grows increasingly rugged, with a mess of rocks, boulders and moraines, while the individual peaks that make up the headwall take on a new dimension. The trail skirts the north side of the Bonne Pierre glacier and crosses a great rocky scoop on the left topped by Tête Sud de la Somme and the Roche d'Alvau. Go as far as you feel comfortable before turning back.

> *Historic note:* It was on the moraine bank of the Bonne Pierre glacier that Whymper, Moore, Walker, Croz and Almer made their bivouac the night before achieving the first ascent of the Barre des Écrins on 25 June 1864. From their bivouac A.W. Moore described seeing 'far, far above us, at an almost inconceivable height … a wonderful rocky pinnacle, bathed in the beams of the fast-sinking sun. We were so electrified by the glory of the sight that it was some seconds before we realized what we saw, and understood that that astounding point, removed apparently miles from the earth, was one of the highest summits of Les Ecrins' (The Alps in 1864).

Route 66: La Bérarde (1713m) – Refuge du Châtelleret (2232m)

Grade:	2
Distance:	5 kilometres (one way)
Height gain:	519 metres
Time:	2–2½hrs (1½hrs down)
Location:	North of La Bérarde

La Bérarde, top mountaineering centre of the Écrins Park (Routes 63–70)

South Face of La Meije from the summit of Tête de la Maye (Route 64)

South Face of La Meije from the Refuge du Châtelleret approach (Route 66)

As they descended the Vallon des Etançons in June 1864 after having made the first crossing of the Brêche de la Meije from La Grave, both the young Edward Whymper and his companion A.W. Moore were scathing in their contempt for the glen. Whymper described it as 'a howling wilderness, the abomination of desolation … suggestive of chaos, but of little else' (Scrambles Amongst the Alps). Moore complained: 'There was no end to it, and we became more savage at every step, unanimously agreeing that no power on earth would ever induce us to walk up or down this particular valley again' (The Alps in 1864). Then he relented. His venom had been directed at the lack of a path which had made the descent so painful, and was forced to admit that: 'The scenery is, nevertheless, … of the highest order of rugged grandeur.'

A path has long been made from La Bérarde to the Châtelleret refuge, built below the South Face of La Meije, so today's walker can make this outing without cause for complaint and enjoy almost every step of the way the 'rugged grandeur' of the scenery. It is, indeed, of the highest order, and this route makes the most of it.

There are two ways to begin this walk: from the signed path which leaves the road about 40m downstream of the bridge at the entrance to La Bérarde (the start of Route 64); or by taking the path alongside the Bureau des Guides building used at the start of Route 65. If using the first option, continue beyond the Tête de la Maye junction, still gaining height across the hillside, then briefly slope downhill to cross a footbridge over the Etançons stream. Continue upvalley among silver birch, alpenrose and low-growing clumps of bilberry to be joined soon after by the alternative path from La Bérarde.

The Bureau des Guides path (Route 65) crosses the Bonne Pierre torrent and forks. This is where the Vallon de Bonne Pierre route branches to the right. Ignore this right-hand option and continue within the main Etançons valley, soon joining the other path mentioned above.

The way now leads through lush beds of juniper and alpenrose, the Etançons stream to the left and waterfalls pouring down cliffs that wall the valley on both sides. Ahead the glen appears to narrow, then curves. As you begin to round this curve, so the majestic Meije rises ahead. It's an awesome sight. The path forks, with the left branch (to Plaret Gény) sloping down to cross the

The South Face of La Meije, seen from the approach route to Refuge Châtelleret (Route 66)

stream before rising in long loops up the opposite hillside. The way to Châtelleret continues ahead, and as you complete the curve you enter the upper valley, where La Meije is seen in all its full sweep of rock and glacier with the refuge below it. Wander through a rocky area, then curve left to cross the Etançons stream on a f o o t b r i d g e . Thereafter it's a straightforward slant upvalley before recrossing the stream just below the **Refuge du Châtelleret** (2232m: *accommodation, refreshments*).

> *Note: The first refuge was built here in the early 1880s (on what Moore had described as 'a perfect oasis … a small plot of scanty grass with loose rocks lying about'), but after 20 years or so it was largely neglected by climbers, who preferred to use the higher Refuge du Promontoire. By the 1950s the Châtelleret was dismissed as being little more than a broken-down, three-walled hovel built against a huge boulder. The present hut, however, is large, snug and accommodating, and capable of sleeping 90 in its dormitories.*

Route 67: La Bérarde (1713m) –
Refuge du Plan du Carrelet (1908m)

Grade:	1
Distance:	3½ kilometres (one way)
Height gain:	195 metres
Time:	1hr (45mins return)
Location:	Southeast of La Bérarde

This is the shortest and easiest walk to be tackled from La Bérarde, a gentle valley stroll to a privately-owned mountain refuge at a junction of valleys.

The route begins by wandering past the large CAF building that houses the Centre Alpin and which covers the track at the southeast end of La Bérarde. Follow the path beyond as it rises gently along the lower vegetated slopes on the left-hand side of the Vénéon torrent. About 10mins from the village you enter the national park and continue with mountain views growing in stature as you progress. After about 50mins the path forks, with one branch going right to cross the river (see Route 68). The trail to the refuge continues ahead, and about 10mins later comes to the small plain on which stands the **Refuge du Plan du Carrelet** (1908m: *accommodation, refreshments*). Across the valley stretches the rugged Vallon du Chardon, and walkers with binoculars are often able to watch chamois within that glen.

Two other refuges may be visited along the upper reaches of the Vénéon beyond the Carrelet: the Temple-Écrins (Route 69) and Pilatte (Route 70).

Route 68: La Bérarde (1713m) – Vallon du
Chardon (2092m) – La Bérarde

Grade:	2–3
Distance:	11 kilometres
Height gain/loss:	395 metres
Time:	4hrs
Location:	South of La Bérarde

Carved from the mountains on the west side of the upper Vénéon opposite the Carrelet refuge, the Vallon du Chardon is a wild but attractive glen, its rubble-strewn glacier fed by higher icefields of a more pristine appearance. The moraines that border the Glacier du Chardon are crowded with Alpine flowers, while chamois and marmots are the sole inhabitants of this untamed wilderness. But those who wander into the glen are rewarded by magnificent views of the Barre des Écrins (perhaps the finest views that walkers will get of this handsome mountain) and of other neighbouring peaks. This walk makes the most of those views. It's a circular route, and although it could be tackled in the opposite direction to that described, this clockwise circuit is the preferred option.

Walk upvalley from La Bérarde following directions to Refuge du Carrelet as given in Route 67 above, but 50mins from La Bérarde (10mins before the hut), where the path forks, bear right on an unsigned trail which crosses a footbridge over the Vénéon torrent at about 1870m. Across the river the path zigzags a short distance up a vegetated slope, then contours to the left (south) with views to the huge rock mass of L'Ailefroide. The way becomes extremely attractive among small birch trees and mattresses of juniper and alpenrose as it leads gently along the lower hillside and brings you to the mouth of the Chardon glen.

About 1½hrs from La Bérarde cross the Chardon torrent on a footbridge where the river battles among massive boulders, then climb quite steeply before angling across the hillside and coming to an unmarked crossing path (about 1895m). Turn right on an easy contour and make your way into the Chardon glen. The valley is walled by a high ridge from which several small glaciers are suspended, and on entering you notice how the vegetation decreases and a more stony wilderness beckons. Before long the path swings to the right and crosses the torrent on another footbridge, from which tremendous views are enjoyed of the Barre des Écrins to the northeast.

Over the bridge turn left for a few paces before cutting back to the right. (**Note:** another minor but cairned path extends further upvalley, leading over old moraine debris to give closer views of the neighbouring peaks and a whole string of cascade ribbons falling from them.) Now rising a little, the path back to La Bérarde cuts along the northern hillside, then rounds the valley's 'gateway' before contouring high above the Vénéon, with Le Râteau looking appealing way to the north at the head of the Etançons glen.

After picking a route across a rocky landslip area where the way is cairned, the path soon resumes, then begins the long and gentle descent towards La Bérarde. The village is finally reached across a bridge leading into the car park.

Route 69: La Bérarde (1713m) – Refuge du Temple-Écrins (2410m)

Grade:	2
Distance:	5½ kilometres (one way)
Height gain:	697 metres
Time:	2½hrs (1½hrs down)
Location:	Southeast of La Bérarde

Despite its sombre, barrack-like appearance, the Temple-Écrins hut enjoys a privileged position, set on a shelf below Pic Coolidge and the Barre des Écrins about 500m above the valley. Views from it are exquisite – to the Glacier de la Pilatte and Les Bans in the south, with the glacier-clad Mont Gioberney to the right of that, and a whole host of shapely mountains in almost every direction. The route to the hut is never overly demanding, but retains interest throughout.

Follow directions as for Route 67 to **Refuge du Plan du Carrelet** (1908m, 1hr: *accommodation, refreshments*) and continue upvalley on the left-hand side of the Vénéon torrent, briefly passing through groves of pine and juniper, and about 10mins beyond the refuge come to a path junction (1935m) with a sign indicating the way left to Temple-Écrins in 1½hrs. This path winds uphill among pines, crosses a ravine with a glacial stream rushing through it, and resumes with numerous zigzags among yet more trees before emerging over a shelf into a hanging valley. At the head of this stands the Barre des Écrins, monarch of the Dauphiné Alps and the Alps' most southerly 4000m peak. Small glaciers, screes and glacier-smoothed slabs form an austere backdrop. Just to the right stands the **Refuge du Temple-Écrins** (2410m: *accommodation, refreshments*), a long, low, flat-roofed stone building.

Route 70: La Bérarde (1713m) – Refuge de la Pilatte (2572m)

Grade:	2
Distance:	8½ kilometres (one way)
Height gain:	859 metres
Time:	3½hrs (2½hrs down)
Location:	SSE of La Bérarde

Perched at the head of the upper Vallée du Vénéon, and with an awe-inspiring full-frontal view of the Glacier de la Pilatte which cascades from Les Bans, the Pilatte refuge enjoys one of the finest outlooks of any hut in the Écrins region. Choose a good-weather day to visit, and spend time there absorbing its memorable location.

Begin as for Route 69, but where the path to the Temple-Écrins refuge breaks left (1935m, 1hr 10mins) continue ahead, soon leaving trees behind and entering a rougher, more stony region, but with Les Bans in sight ahead, its glacial bulk blocking the valley in a gleam of ice and rock. The landscape becomes more wild and untamed, and at 2163m the trail crosses to the west side of the valley by footbridge, then resumes by climbing in zigzags towards the south. Ahead you should be able to see a rain gauge set upon a big slab shoulder of hillside. This is a good indicator of how far and how much higher you have still to go, because the refuge (unseen from here) stands just beyond it.

Cross a shallow cirque in which the Glacier du Says hangs between Mont Gioberney and the Pics du Says, and another plank footbridge takes you across the glacier's drainage stream. Now the path twists up the lateral moraine which banks the Glacier de la Pilatte, and at the top you pass the rain gauge seen earlier. Just ahead stands the **Refuge de la Pilatte** (2572m: *accommodation, refreshments*), a large, sturdy and well-equipped hut. Allow 2½hrs to return to La Bérarde by the same path.

Other Walks from La Bérarde

• On the way to the Châtelleret refuge (Route 66) the path forks halfway along the Vallon des Étançons. While the path to the hut continues ahead, the alternative trail veers left, crosses the stream and climbs the western hillside under the Glacier du Plaret. From this hillside (signed to **PLARET GÉNY**) you gain a splendid overview of the valley, the Meije at its head and the eastern walling mountains.

- South of La Bérarde a steeply climbing path takes you onto the slopes of the **GRANDE AIGUILLE DE LA BÉRARDE**. By taking this path to a little over 2500m more impressive views will be obtained – similar to, though not as extensive as, those from the Tête de la Maye.

- Finally, it's possible to walk downvalley to **BOURG D'OISANS** following footpaths almost all the way, and with an incredible range of both scenery and vegetation to experience. Allow at least two days for this.

APPENDIX A

Tour of the Oisans: GR54

On a number of occasions in this guide references have been made to the classic multi-day trek which works a circuit of the Écrins region. GR54 is one of the great Alpine walks, with a succession of stimulating high mountain views to enliven practically every one of its ten stages, and plenty of opportunities to stray into neighbouring glens – given sufficient time and energy, that is. Amounting to a little over 190km, it's of similar length to the better-known Tour of Mont Blanc, but is, however, a rather more challenging proposition with some fairly tough stages and a number of long, steep climbs in order to gain lofty passes. Cicerone Press publish a guide to this trek, *Tour of the Oisans: GR54*, by Andrew Harper, while most of the individual stages are included as day walks in the present guide, for each one has much to commend it.

Inaugurated in the mid-1960s, the Tour is generally accepted as starting and ending in Bourg d'Oisans at the western end of the Vallée de la Romanche, from where it makes an initial two-day traverse of the rolling country on the north side of the valley, at the end of which it descends to La Grave at the foot of La Meije **(Route 1)**.

On Day 3 the route follows the Romanche upstream to Refuge de l'Alpe de Villar d'Arène, continues to Col d'Arsine then descends the eastern side of the pass to Le Casset in the Vallée de la Guisane **(Routes 14 and 22)**.

After leaving Le Casset, the Tour of the Oisans veers away from the Guisane and climbs through forest and over open hillsides to gain Col de l'Eychauda. There follows a long descent to the Vallée de la Vallouise **(Route 24)**, where one could either divert to Ailefroide, or continue through the valley as far as Vallouise.

Above and to the west of Vallouise lies the tributary valley of the Onde which carries GR54 to Entre les Aygues. From there it strikes south then southwest through the narrow Vallon de la Selle on a long and demanding stage which crosses two passes (Col de l'Aup Martin and Pas de la Cavale) before dropping to Refuge du Pré de la Chaumette in a charming pastoral setting at the south-ernmost point of the circuit **(Route 25)**.

A little longer even than the previous stage, on Day 6 the trek tackles three cols in quick succession to cross ridge systems projecting from Le Sirac. Refuge de Vallonpierre is briefly visited on the descent to the Valgaudemar, and on reaching the bed of the valley the way passes alongside another hut, Refuge du Clot, before taking a streamside path to La Chapelle-en-Valgaudemar **(Routes 39 and 40)**.

An easy stroll downstream to Villar Loubiere, followed by an abrupt turn to the north, takes the route up to the 2500m Col de la Vaurze, then a sharp 1200m descent plunges GR54 down to the attractive little village of Le Désert **(Route 48)** in the Valjouffrey. Valjouffrey is narrow at this point, but a grassy ravine on its northern side makes an indent of the mountain wall which gives access to Col de Côte Belle by which the walk crosses to Valsenestre **(Route 49)** on Day 8.

The penultimate stage is a 7–8hr delight (described as **Route 50**), crossing the 2625m Col de la Muzelle, with a lengthy descent via the Lac and Refuge de la Muzelle to Bourg d'Arud in the Vallée du Vénéon. A final, easy valley stroll leads back to Bourg d'Oisans where the Tour of the Oisans began.

APPENDIX B

Notes on Selected Peaks of the Écrins Region

AIGUILLE DIBONA (3131m)

An impressive granite needle standing proud of the Massif du Soreiller at the head of the gorge-like Soreiller glen, the Aiguille boasts numerous routes easily reached from the popular STD refuge which stands at its base. Originally called the Pain de Sucre, the blade-like Aiguille was later renamed following a protracted correspondence between activists from France, Britain and Austria. It was first climbed via the north ridge by Guido Meyer and Angelo Dibona in June 1913.

LES BANS (3669m)

With the rippling curtain of the Glacier de la Pilatte hanging down its north face, Les Bans gazes down the upper Vallée du Vénéon, a great bulk of a mountain commanding three separate valleys. The 1100m west face overlooks the Valgaudemar, while the southeastern side forms a headwall to the Vallée de l'Onde above Entre les Aygues. W.A.B. Coolidge made the first ascent in 1878 by the ENE ridge with Christian Almer, father and son, as his guides. Their route is now considered the easiest on the mountain (grade PD), from which the views are said to be magnificent.

BARRE DES ÉCRINS (4102m)

The most southerly 4000m peak in the Alps, the Barre des Écrins is dominated on its northern side by the cascading Glacier Blanc, while the south flank consists almost entirely of rock – the 1100m South Pillar here is one of the great rock climbs of the region. Unlike the Meije, which is conspicuous from numerous viewpoints, the Barre des Écrins is largely hidden, and the only road from which it is properly viewed runs up the south side of Col du Galibier. First climbed in June 1864 by Edward Whymper, A.W. Moore, Horace Walker and the guides Michel Croz and Christian Almer, after a bivouac in the Vallon de la Bonne Pierre above La Bérarde, the ascent was recorded in *Scrambles Amongst the Alps* (by Whymper) and *The Alps in 1864* (by Moore). Whymper's account included a description, accompanied by the now-famous illustration, of 'Almer's Leap', which years later was discounted by the pedantic Alpine historian W.A.B. Coolidge – himself a pioneer of the Dauphiné Alps. The dispute degenerated into one of the most public arguments in mountaineering history.

LA MEIJE (3982m)

'One can hardly speak in exaggerated terms of its jagged ridges, torrential glaciers, and tremendous precipices,' wrote Whymper in *Scrambles*, and speaking for a later generation R.L.G. Irving said: 'The huge rock wall that forms the south face of the Meije as it is seen at the head of the Etançons glen ... is a thing to rejoice a climber's heart, but it is far less beautiful than the thousands of feet of ice-hung precipice that hold every eye in every car as it approaches La Grave.' Whether viewed from the north above La Grave or from the Etançons glen in the south, the Meije is not only one of the finest mountains in the Écrins, but it ranks among the most respected in all the Alps. Previously known as the Aiguille du Midi de la Grave, the Meije drew the attention of some of the leading alpinists of the 19th century. In 1870 W.A.B. Coolidge reached the Pic Central, only to discover that to the west another peak (the Grand Pic) was slightly higher. 'We had some thoughts of trying it,' wrote Coolidge later, 'but Almer [Christian Almer, his guide] pronounced it utterly impossible for any human being to reach the summit, as it was sheer on all sides.' Other parties tried and failed, until the 20-year-old Boileau de Castelnau with Pierre Gaspard, father and son from St-Christophe, finally succeeded on 16 August 1877 after a bivouac near the site of the present Châtelleret refuge. The account of that ascent includes the following passage: 'The rocks by which we reached the little upper glacier of the Meije, or Glacier du Doigt, and the last metres of the ascent are of unheard of difficulty. It will be enough to say that we remained nearly two hours, seven or eight metres from the top without being able to reach it, and we were nearly forced to beat a retreat at this spot.' Today the mountain offers numerous quality rock climbs on both north and south faces, while the west–east traverse of the cock's-comb summit ridge from the Grand Pic to Pic Central has long been considered an Alpine classic. This traverse was first achieved in 1885 by the noted Austrian team of the Zsigmondy brothers, Emil and Otto, with Ludwig Purtscheller, but in 1964 the nature of the route changed somewhat when the Brèche Zsigmondy collapsed. Two weeks after their successful traverse, Emil Zsigmondy was killed whilst attempting a new route on the same peak.

L'OLAN (3564m)

Looming large on the north side of the Valgaudemar opposite La Chapelle, this great block of a mountain with twin summits is recognisable from several distant points, although its profile varies. While the standard route climbs the southeast face, the northwest wall above the Fond Turbat refuge is 1100m high and split by a central couloir. The wall was first climbed over two days in August 1934 by Devies and Gervasutti. On the other side of the central couloir, over a three-day period in 1956, Couzy and Desmaison created another classic, a direct route that was not repeated for ten years. These two routes are among the most exacting on the mountain. On the north side of the Olan, on a ridge leading to the Aiguille de l'Olan, the 2970m Brèche de l'Olan is used as a link between the Fond Turbat and Lavey huts and was first crossed in the 1870s.

MONT PELVOUX (3943m)

This massive, prominent mountain with several summits was long regarded as the highest in the Dauphiné Alps. The secondary summit of Pointe Durand (3932m) was climbed as early as 1828 by a party of military surveyors, and the main peak was reached 20 years later by the astronomer Victor Puiseux, whose name has been applied to it. The mountain stands at a confluence of valleys above the climbing centre of Ailefroide in the Vallée de la Vallouise. A group of small cirque glaciers adorn its upper southern slopes, while the long stream of the Glacier Noir flows down its northern flank. On his way to Ailefroide to climb the mountain in 1861 (on only his second visit to the Alps), the young Edward Whymper commented that 'the whole height of the peak which in these valleys goes under the name of the "Grand Pelvoux" is seen at one glance from summit to base, six or seven thousand feet of nearly perpendicular cliffs.' A very fine impression can be gained of the south face from the Bosse de Clapouse.

APPENDIX C

Useful Addresses

1: Tourist Information

French Government Tourist Office
178 Piccadilly
LONDON W1V 0AL
(☎ 0891 244 123)
Websites:
http://www.franceguide.com
http://www.fr-holidaystore.co.uk

French Government Tourist Office
38 Lower Abbey Street
DUBLIN 1
(☎ 1 703 4046)

French Government Tourist Office
610 Fifth Avenue
NEW YORK
NY 10020-2452
Website: www.info.france-usa.org

Rail Europe Travel Centre
179 Piccadilly
LONDON W1V 0BA
(☎ 0990 848 848; calls charged at the
national rate)

Comité Régional du Tourisme
Rhône-Alpes
104 route de Paris
69260 CHARBONNIERES-LES-BAINS
(☎ 04 72 59 21 59)

Comité départemental du Tourisme
des Hautes-Alpes
Immeuble 'Le Relais'
5ter, rue Capitaine de Bresson
05000 GAP
(☎ 04 92 53 62 00)

Comité départemental du Tourisme
de l'Isère
14, rue de la République
BP 227
38019 GRENOBLE Cedex
(☎ 04 76 54 34 36)

Maison du Tourisme
Bureau Information Montagne
38019 GRENOBLE
(☎ 04 76 42 45 90)

2: National Park Information

Parc National des Écrins (Head Office)
Domaine de Charance
05000 GAP
(☎ 04 92 40 20 10)
E-mail: ecrins-parcnational@
espaces-naturels.fr

Secteur du Briançonnais
Maison du Parc
Place Médecin-Général Blanchard
05100 BRIANÇON
(☎ 04 92 21 08 49)

Secteur de la Vallouise
Maison du Parc
05290 VALLOUISE
(☎ 04 92 23 32 31)

Secteur de l'Embrunais
Maison du Parc
Place de l'Eglise
05380 CHATEAUROUX
(☎ 04 92 43 23 31)

Secteur du Champsaur
Maison de la Vallée
05260 PONT-DU-FOSSÉ
(☎ 04 92 55 95 44)

Secteur du Valgaudemar
Maison du Parc
05800 LA CHAPELLE-EN-
    VALGAUDEMAR
(☎ 04 92 55 25 19)

Secteur du Valbonnais
Maison du Parc
38740 ENTRAIGUES
(☎ 04 76 30 20 61)

Secteur de l'Oisans
Maison du Parc
Rue Gambetta
BP 47
38520 BOURG D'OISANS
(☎ 04 76 80 00 51)

3: French Alpine Club
Club Alpin Français
24 avénue de la Laumière
75019 PARIS

4: Map Suppliers
Edward Stanford Ltd
12–14 Long Acre
LONDON WC2E 9BR
(☎ 0207 836 1321)

The Map Shop
15 High Street
UPTON-UPON-SEVERN
WR8 0HJ

World Leisure Marketing
11 Newmarket Court
Newmarket Drive
DERBY DE24 8NW
(☎ 01332 573737)

IGN Shop
107 rue la Baetie
75008 PARIS

Ulysse
4176 St-Denis
MONTREAL
Quebec H2W 2M5

Rand McNally Map Store
10 East 53rd Street
NEW YORK
NY

Map Link Inc
30 South La Patera Lane
Unit #5
SANTA BARBARA
California 93117

5: Specialist Mountain Activities Insurance
(AAC members only)
Austrian Alpine Club
2 Church Road
WELWYN GARDEN CITY
AL8 6PT
(☎ 01707 324835)
(membership carries automatic accident and rescue insurance)

(BMC members only)
BMC Travel and Activity Insurance
177–179 Burton Road
MANCHESTER M20 2BB
(☎ 0161 445 4747)

Harrison Beaumont Ltd
2 Des Roches Square
WITNEY OX8 6BE
(☎ 01993 700200)

Snowcard Insurance Services
Lower Boddington
DAVENTRY NN11 6BR
(☎ 01327 262805)

APPENDIX D

Metric Conversions

1: Length and Area

To convert *to* metric, multiply by the factor shown. For conversions *from* metric to imperial, divide by the same factor.

	multiply by
miles to kilometres	1.6093
yards to metres	0.9144
feet to metres	0.3048
inches to centimetres	2.54
acres to hectares	0.4047

Equivalent distances/areas

Kilometres		Miles
0.5	=	0.3
1.0	=	0.6
1.6	=	1.0
2.0	=	1.2
5.0	=	3.1
8.0	=	5.0

Hectares		Acres
1	=	2.47

Metres		Feet
100	=	328
300	=	984
500	=	1640
1000	=	3281
1500	=	4921
2000	=	6562
2500	=	8202
3000	=	9843
3500	=	11483
4000	=	13123

2: Temperature

To convert Celsius to Fahrenheit, divide by 5, then multiply the result by 9, and add 32.

To convert Fahrenheit to Celsius, subtract 32, divide the result by 9, and multiply by 5.

Celsius		Fahrenheit
0	=	32
10	=	50
20	=	68
30	=	86

3: Liquid Capacity

To convert *to* metric, multiply by the factor given. To convert *from* metric, divide by the factor.

	multiply by
gallons to litres	4.546
pints to litres	0.568

Litres		Gallons	Litres		Pints
1	=	0.22	0.5	=	0.88
2	=	0.44	1.0	=	1.76
3	=	0.66	1.5	=	2.64
4	=	0.88	2.0	=	3.52
5	=	1.10	5.0	=	8.8

4: Weight

To convert *to* metric, multiply by the factor shown. For conversions *from* metric, divide by the factor.

	multiply by
ounces to grams	28.3495
pounds to kilograms	0.4536

Grams		Ounces	Kilograms		Pounds
28.35	=	1	0.5	=	1.10
56.69	=	2	1.0	=	2.20
141.74	=	5	5.0	=	11.00
			10.0	=	22.00

APPENDIX E

English–French Glossary

accommodation	logement	crest (ridge)	crête
accommodation list	guide des hébergements	dam	barrage
		dangerous	dangereux
bakery	boulangerie, dépôt de pain	dinner	dîner
		dormitory	dortoir
bank	banque	eagle	aigle
barn	grange	east	est
bath	bain	easy	facile
bedroom	chambre	exchange (currency)	échange
beer (draft beer)	bière (bière pression)	fine weather	beau temps
		footpath	sentier, chemin
blister	ampoule	forbidden	défense de
boots	chaussures de montagne	forest	forêt
breakfast	petit déjeuner	free	libre
bread	pain	full	complet
bridge (footbridge)	pont (passerelle)	full board	pension complète
		grocery	épicerie, alimentation
bus	autobus, autocar	half-board (half-pension)	demi pension
bus station	gare routière		
bus stop	arrêt autocar	hamlet	hameau
butcher	boucher	help	secours
cable-car	téléphérique	hill	colline
cairn	cairn	hotel list	liste d'hôtels
campsite	le camping, terrain de camping	hour	heure
		hut-keeper	gardien
chairlift	télésiège	hydro-electric works	usine hydro electrique
chamois	chamois		
chapel	chapelle	ibex	bouquetin
chemist	pharmacie	ice	glace
church	église	ice axe	piolet
closed	fermé	information	information, renseignements
cloud (cloudy)	nuage (nuageux)		
cold	froid	lake	lac
compass	boussole	left (direction)	gauche

lightning	éclair	shower	douche
lower, or under	dessous	shuttle (bus)	navette
lunch	déjeuner	sleeping bag	sac de couchage
map	carte	snack bar	buvette
marmot	marmotte	snow	neige
mill	moulin	south	sud
mountain	montagne	spring (of water)	source, fontaine
mountain bike	vélo tout terrain/	stonefall	chute de pierres
	VTT	storm	tempête, orage
mountain hut	refuge	stream	ruisseau
mountain inn	chalet-refuge	sunny	ensoleillé, du soleil
mountain rescue	secours en	sunstroke	coup de soleil
	montagne	supermarket	supermarché
mountain stream	torrent	telephone card	télécarte
national park	Maison du Park	thunder	tonnerre
information office		timetable	horaire
north	nord	tourist office	office du tourisme,
occupied (toilet)	occupé		syndicat d'initiative
open	ouvert	train	train
outdoor activities	activités de	upper	dessus
	plein air	valley	val, vallée, vallon
pass	col	via/over	via/par-dessus
pasture	pâturage	walking guide	accompagnateur
railway	chemin de fer	warm	chaud
railway station	gare	water	eau
rain	pluie	waymark	balisage
reservoir	réservoir	weather forecast	météo
ridge	arête	west	ouest
right (direction)	droit	wind	vent
room	chambre	woodland	bois
rope	corde	youth hostel	auberge de jeunesse
round trip	aller-retour		
rucksack	sac à dos		
scree	éboulis	**Acronyms**	
section	tronçon	CAF	Club Alpin Française
sheet sleeping bag	sac à viande	PTT	Poste, Téléphone,
shelter	abri		Télégraphe (Post Office)
shepherd's hut	bergerie	STD	Société des Touristes du
shop	magasin		Dauphiné

BIBLIOGRAPHY

Although there are many excellent books in French devoted to the Dauphiné Alps in general and the Parc National des Écrins in particular, the following list is restricted to English-language titles. It is a selective list, and some of those included are out of print. However, they should be obtainable by special request from public libraries.

1: General Tourist Guides

There are numerous general tourist guides to France which include brief items related to the Écrins region, but the following are more specifically mountain oriented.

Michelin Tourist Guide: French Alps – Published in 1998 as part of the well-known Michelin Green Guide Series, this title covers the whole of the Alpine range in France from Lake Geneva to the Alpes Maritime. Useful items relating to the Écrins National Park region are included.

The Outdoor Traveler's Guide: The Alps by Marcia R. Lieberman (Stewart, Tabori & Chang, New York, 1991) Lavishly illustrated with colour photographs by Tim Thompson, this makes a good Alpine primer, with short essays on many regions of the Alps. Coverage includes the Écrins.

2: Mountains and Mountaineering

Ecrins Massif by John Brailsford (Alpine Club, London, 1987) A climbing guidebook to selected routes by a professional guide now based in the Écrins region.

Ecrins Park by Robin G. Collomb (West Col, Goring, 1986) Another mainly climbing guide devoted to the same area, but with a selection of outline walking routes included.

The Mountains of Europe by Kev Reynolds (Oxford Illustrated Press, Oxford, 1990) Includes a chapter by John Brailsford devoted to Dauphiné, with good background material on the Écrins.

Scrambles Amongst the Alps by Edward Whymper (John Murray – various editions) Although best known for the story of Whymper's attempts and final success on the Matterhorn, *Scrambles* also describes his 1861 ascent of Mont Pelvoux and his subsequent crossing of the Brêche de la Meije, first ascent of the Barre des Écrins and traverse of the Col de la Pilatte in 1864.

The Alps in 1864 by A.W. Moore (latest edition pb Blackwell, 1939) Moore was in the Écrins with Whymper and Horace Walker in the summer of 1864, and his book includes his account of the expeditions outlined above.

3: Walking

Walking the Alpine Parks of France & Northwest Italy by Marcia R. Lieberman (The Mountaineers, Seattle/Cordee, Leicester, 1994) Includes a selection of day walks within the Écrins National Park.

Walking in the Alps by Kev Reynolds (Cicerone Press, Milnthorpe, 1998) Covering the whole range from the Alpes Maritime to the Julian Alps, a section is devoted to the Écrins.

Tour of the Oisans: GR54 by Andrew Harper (Cicerone Press, Milnthorpe – 2nd ed. 1995) A walking guide to this challenging circuit by the author of the well-known guide to the Tour of Mont Blanc.

Classic Walks in Europe by Walt Unsworth (Oxford Illustrated Press, Oxford, 1987) An inspiring book for the adventurous walker, a chapter by Andrew Harper is devoted to the Tour of the Oisans.

Walking & Climbing in the Alps by Stefano Ardito (Swan Hill Press, Shrewsbury, 1994) This glossy hardback is a translation from the original Italian. Describing a number of multi-day tours in the Alps, it includes an eight-day walk from St-Véran in the Queyras to La Grave at the foot of La Meije.

ROUTE INDEX

MAP INDEX

CICERONE GUIDES

WALKING AND TREKKING IN THE ALPS

WALKING IN THE ALPS
Kev Reynolds

The popular author of many of our Alpine guidebooks now draws on his vast experience to produce an outstanding comprehensive volume. Every area covered. Not for over half a century has there been anything remotely comparable. Fully illustrated.
ISBN 1 85284 261 X Large format Case bound 496pp

100 HUT WALKS IN THE ALPS
Kev Reynolds

A fine introduction to Europe's highest mountains and to life in the excellent network of Alpine huts. From southern France, through Switzerland, Austria and Italy to Slovenia. Printed in full colour.
ISBN 1 85284 297 0

CHAMONIX TO ZERMATT - The Walker's Haute Route
Kev Reynolds

The classic walk in the shadow of great peaks from Mont Blanc to the Matterhorn. In 14 stages, this is one of the most beautiful LD paths in Europe.
ISBN 1 85284 215 6 176pp

THE GRAND TOUR OF MONTE ROSA
C.J. Wright

The ultimate alpine LD walk which encircles most of the Pennine Alps.

Vol 1: MARTIGNY TO VALLE DELLA SESIA (via the Italian valleys)
ISBN 1 85284 177 X 216pp PVC cover

Vol 2: VALLE DELLA SESIA TO MARTIGNY (via the Swiss valleys)
ISBN 1 85284 178 8 182pp PVC cover

TOUR OF MONT BLANC
Andrew Harper

One of the world's best walks - the circumnavigation of the Mont Blanc massif. 120 miles of pure magic, split into 11 sections. Reprinted and updated.
ISBN 1 85284 240 7 144pp PVC cover

FRANCE, BELGIUM AND LUXEMBOURG

WALKING IN THE ARDENNES
Alan Castle

53 circular walks in this attractive area of gorges and deep-cut wooded valleys, caves, castles and hundreds of walking trails. Easily accessible from the channel.
ISBN 1 85284 213 X 312pp

SELECTED ROCK CLIMBS IN BELGIUM AND LUXEMBOURG
Chris Craggs

Perfect rock, good protection and not too hot to climb in summer.
ISBN 1 85284 155 9 188p A5

THE BRITTANY COASTAL PATH
Alan Castle

The GR34, 360 miles, takes a month to walk. Easy access from UK means it can be split into several holidays.
ISBN 1 85284 185 0 296pp

CHAMONIX - MONT BLANC - A Walking Guide
Martin Collins

In the dominating presence of Europe's highest mountain, the scenery is exceptional. A comprehensive guide to the area.
ISBN 1 85284 009 9 192pp PVC cover

GR20: THE CORSICAN HIGH LEVEL ROUTE
Paddy Dillon

A new book for this very popular route along the most challenging of the French LD paths - across the rocky spine of Corsica.
ISBN 1 85284 321 7 PVC cover (due 2001)

WALKING THE FRENCH ALPS: GR5
Martin Collins

CICERONE GUIDES

The popular trail from Lake Geneva to Nice. Split into stages, each of which could form the basis of a good holiday.
ISBN 1 85284 051 X 160pp PVC cover

WALKING THE FRENCH GORGES
Alan Castle

320 miles through Provence and Ardèche. Includes the famous gorges of the Verdon.
ISBN 1 85284 114 1 224pp

FRENCH ROCK
Bill Birkett

THE guide to many exciting French crags! Masses of photo topos, with selected hit-routes in detail.
ISBN 1 85284 113 3 332pp A5 size

WALKING IN THE HAUTE SAVOIE
Janette Norton

61 walks in the pre-Alps of Chablais, to majestic peaks in the Faucigny, Haut Giffre and Lake Annecy regions.
ISBN 1 85284 196 6 312pp

WALKING IN THE LANGUEDOC
John Cross

31 walks in the stunningly beautiful Parc Naturel du Haut-Languedoc. The climate is warm, the vineyards stretch out below you, and above is the towering Massif.
ISBN 1 85284 309 8 (due 2001)

TOUR OF THE OISANS: GR54
Andrew Harper

This popular walk around the Dauphiné massif and Écrins national park is similar in quality to the celebrated Tour of Mont Blanc. A two-week suggested itinerary covers the 270km route.
ISBN 1 85284 157 5 120pp PVC cover

WALKING IN PROVENCE
Janette Norton

42 walks through the great variety of Provence - remote plateaux, leafy gorges, ancient villages, monuments, quiet towns. Provence is evocative of a gentler life.
ISBN 1 85284 293 8 248pp

THE PYRENEAN TRAIL: GR10
Alan Castle

From the Atlantic to the Mediterranean at a lower level than the Pyrenean High Route. 50 days - but splits into holiday sections.
ISBN 1 85284 245 8 176pp

THE TOUR OF THE QUEYRAS
Alan Castle

A 13-day walk which traverses wild but beautiful country, the sunniest part of the French Alps. Suitable for a first Alpine visit.
ISBN 1 85284 048 X 160pp

THE ROBERT LOUIS STEVENSON TRAIL
Alan Castle

140 mile trail in the footsteps of Stevenson's *Travels with a Donkey* through the Cevennes from Le Puy to St Jean du Gard. This route is ideal for people new to walking holidays.
ISBN 1 85284 060 9 160pp

WALKING IN THE TARENTAISE AND BEAUFORTAIN ALPS
J.W. Akitt

The delectable mountain area south of Mont Blanc includes the Vanoise National Park. 53 day walks, 5 tours between 2 and 8 days' duration, plus 40 short outings.
ISBN 1 85284 181 8 216pp

ROCK CLIMBS IN THE VERDON - An Introduction
Rick Newcombe

An English-style guide, which makes for easier identification of the routes and descents.
ISBN 1 85284 015 3 72pp

TOUR OF THE VANOISE
Kev Reynolds

A 10-12 day circuit of one of the finest mountain areas of France, between Mt Blanc and the Écrins. The second most popular mountain tour after the Tour of Mont Blanc.
ISBN 1 85284 224 5 120pp

CICERONE GUIDES

WALKS IN VOLCANO COUNTRY   *Alan Castle*
Two LD walks in Central France, the High Auvergne and Tour of the Velay, in a unique landscape of extinct volcanoes.
ISBN 1 85284 092 7 208pp

FRANCE/SPAIN

ROCK CLIMBS IN THE PYRENEES   *Derek Walker*
Includes Pic du Midi d'Ossau and the Vignemale in France, and the Ordesa Canyon and Riglos in Spain.
ISBN 1 85284 039 0 168pp PVC cover

WALKS AND CLIMBS IN THE PYRENEES   *Kev Reynolds*
Includes the Pyrenean High Level Route. Invaluable for any backpacker or mountaineer who plans to visit this still unspoilt mountain range. (3rd Edition)
ISBN 1 85284 133 8 328pp PVC cover

THE WAY OF ST JAMES: Le Puy to Santiago - A Cyclist's Guide   *John Higginson*
This guide for touring cyclists follows as closely as possible the original route but avoids the almost unrideable sections of the walkers' way. On surfaced lanes and roads.
ISBN 1 85284 274 1 112pp

THE WAY OF ST JAMES: Le Puy to Santiago - A Walker's Guide   *Alison Raju*
A walker's guide to the ancient route of pilgrimage. Plus the continuation to Finisterre.
ISBN 1 85284 271 7 264pp

SPAIN AND PORTUGAL

WALKING IN THE ALGARVE   *June Parker*
The author of *Walking in Mallorca* turns her expert attention to the Algarve, with a selection of walks to help the visitor explore the true countryside.
ISBN 1 85284 173 7 168pp

ANDALUSIAN ROCK CLIMBS   *Chris Craggs*
El Chorro and El Torcal are world famous. Includes Tenerife.
ISBN 1 85284 109 5 168pp

COSTA BLANCA ROCK   *Chris Craggs*
Over 1500 routes on over 40 crags, many for the first time in English. The most comprehensive guide to the area.
ISBN 1 85284 241 5 264pp

MOUNTAIN WALKS ON THE COSTA BLANCA   *Bob Stansfield*
An easily accessible winter walking paradise to rival Mallorca. With rugged limestone peaks and warm climate. This guide includes the 150 km Costa Blanca Mountain Way.
ISBN 1 85284 165 6 232pp

ROCK CLIMBS IN MALLORCA, IBIZA AND TENERIFE   *Chris Craggs*
A new edition of this guide to holiday island cragging at its best.
ISBN 1 85284 319 5 240pp

WALKING IN MALLORCA   *June Parker*
The 3rd edition of this great classic guide takes account of rapidly changing conditions.
ISBN 1 85284 250 4 288pp PVC cover

BIRDWATCHING IN MALLORCA   *Ken Stoba*
A complete guide to what to see and where to see it.
ISBN 1 85284 053 6 108pp

CICERONE GUIDES

THE MOUNTAINS OF CENTRAL SPAIN   *Jaqueline Oglesby*
   Walks and scrambles in the Sierras de Gredos and Guadarrama which rise to 2600m and remain
   snow-capped for 5 months of the year.
   ISBN 1 85284 203 2 312p

THROUGH THE SPANISH PYRENEES: GR11 2nd Edition   *Paul Lucia*
   An updated edition of the long distance trail which mirrors the French GR10 but traverses much
   lonelier, wilder country. With new maps and information.
   ISBN 1 85284 307 1 232pp

WALKING IN THE SIERRA NEVADA   *Andy Walmsley*
   Spain's highest mountain range is a wonderland for the traveller and wilderness backpacker alike.
   Mountainbike routes indicated.
   ISBN 1 85284 194 X 160pp

WALKS AND CLIMBS IN THE PICOS DE EUROPA   *Robin Walker*
   A definitive guide to these unique mountains. Walks and rock climbs of all grades.
   ISBN 1 85284 033 1 232pp PVC cover

SWITZERLAND

ALPINE PASS ROUTE, SWITZERLAND   *Kev Reynolds*
   Over 15 passes along the northern edge of the Alps, past the Eiger, Jungfrau and many other
   renowned peaks. A 325 km route in 15 suggested stages.
   ISBN 1 85284 069 2 176pp

THE BERNESE ALPS, SWITZERLAND   *Kev Reynolds*
   Walks around Grindelwald, Lauterbrunnen and Kandersteg dominated by the great peaks of the
   Oberland.
   ISBN 1 85284 243 1 248pp PVC cover

CENTRAL SWITZERLAND - A Walking Guide   *Kev Reynolds*
   A little known but delightful area stretching from Luzern to the St Gotthard. Includes Engelberg and
   Klausen Pass.
   ISBN 1 85284 131 1 216pp PVC cover

WALKS IN THE ENGADINE, SWITZERLAND   *Kev Reynolds*
   The superb region to the south-east of Switzerland of the Bregaglia, Bernina Alps and the Engadine
   National Park.
   ISBN 1 85284 003 X 192pp PVC cover

THE JURA: WALKING THE HIGH ROUTE and WINTER SKI TRAVERSES
   Kev Reynolds, R. Brian Evans
   The High Route is a long distance path along the highest crest of the Swiss Jura. In winter it is a
   paradise for cross-country skiers. Both sections in one volume.
   ISBN 1 85284 010 2 192pp

WALKING IN TICINO, SWITZERLAND   *Kev Reynolds*
   Walks in the lovely Italian part of Switzerland, surprisingly little known to British walkers.
   ISBN 1 85284 098 6 184pp PVC cover

THE VALAIS, SWITZERLAND - A Walking Guide   *Kev Reynolds*
   The splendid scenery of the Pennine Alps, with such peaks as the Matterhorn, Dent Blanche and
   Mont Rosa providing a perfect background.
   ISBN 1 85284 151 6 224pp PVC cover

CICERONE GUIDES

GERMANY, AUSTRIA AND EASTERN EUROPE

MOUNTAIN WALKING IN AUSTRIA   *Cecil Davies*
An enlarged second edition. 25 mountain groups, 98 walks from half a day to a week.
ISBN 1 85284 239 3 216pp

WALKING IN THE BAVARIAN ALPS   *Grant Bourne and Sabine Korner-Bourne*
57 walks of variety in the Allgäu, Ammergau, Wetterstein, Tegernsee, Chiemgau and Berchtesgaden Alps on the German-Austrian border.
ISBN 1 85284 229 6 184pp

WALKING IN THE BLACK FOREST   *Fleur and Colin Speakman*
Above the Rhine valley, the Ortenauer Wine Path (64km) and the Clock Carriers Way (10 day circular walk) are described, together with practical walking advice for the area in general.
ISBN 1 85284 050 1 120pp

GERMANY'S ROMANTIC ROAD A Guide for Walkers and Cyclists   *Gordon McLachlan*
423 km past historic walled towns and castles of southern Germany.
ISBN 1 85284 233 4 208pp

WALKING IN THE HARZ MOUNTAINS   *Fleur & Colin Speakman*
30 walks in Germany's most northerly mountains, some from the narrow-gauge steam railway.
ISBN 1 85284 149 4 152pp

KING LUDWIG WAY   *Fleur and Colin Speakman*
Travels the Bavarian countryside from Munich to Füssen. King Ludwig was responsible for the fabulous castle of Neuschwanstein and sponsored Wagner's operas.
ISBN 0 902363 90 5 80pp

KLETTERSTEIG - Scrambles in the Northern Limestone Alps
Paul Werner Translated by Dieter Pevsner
Protected climbing paths similar to the Via Ferrata in the German/Austrian border region.
ISBN 0 902363 46 8 184pp PVC cover

THE MOUNTAINS OF ROMANIA   *James Roberts*
A definitive guide to the newly accessible Carpathian mountains. Potentially one of the best walking destinations in Europe, with mountain wilderness and friendly people.
ISBN 1 85284 295 4 296pp

WALKING THE RIVER RHINE TRAIL   *Alan Castle*
A spectacular 170 mile (273 km) walk along Germany's most famous river from Bonn to Alsheim near Worms. Excellent public transport assists the walker.
ISBN 1 85284 276 8 176pp

WALKING IN THE SALZKAMMERGUT   *Fleur and Colin Speakman*
Holiday rambles in Austria's Lake District. Renowned for its historic salt mines.
ISBN 1 85284 030 7 104pp

HUT TO HUT IN THE STUBAI ALPS   *Allan Hartley*
The Stubai Rucksack Route and The Stubai Glacier Tour, each around 10 days. Easy peaks and good huts make it a good area for a first Alpine season.
ISBN 1 85284 123 0 128pp

THE HIGH TATRAS   *Colin Saunders & Renata Narozna*
A detailed guide to the Tatras, a deservedly popular area between Poland and Slovakia.
ISBN 1 85284 150 8 248pp PVC cover